Christmas Breakthrough

Finding the Real Gifts of the Season

Phil Needham
Photography by Holly Needham

CREST
BOOKS

Copyright © 2019 by The Salvation Army

Published by Crest Books

Crest Books
The Salvation Army National Headquarters
615 Slaters Lane
Alexandria, VA 22313
Phone: 703/684-5523

Lt. Col. Tim Foley, *National Program Secretary and Editor-in-Chief*
Lt. Col. Allen Satterlee, *Editor-in-Chief and National Literary Secretary (Retired)*
Roger O. Selvage Jr., *Art Director*
Daniel Schwarz, *Editorial Assistant*
Ashley C. Schena, *Graphic Designer*

ISBN: 978-1-946709-08-0

Printed in the United States of America on acid-free paper.

All rights reserved. No part of this publication may be reproduced, stored in a retrieval system, or transmitted in any form or by any means without prior written permission of the publisher. Exceptions are brief quotations in printed reviews.

Scripture quotations are from the Common English Bible. Copyright © 2011 by the Common English Bible. All rights reserved. Used by permission. www.CommonEnglishBible.com.

Contents

THE IMPORTANCE OF THE ADVENT-CHRISTMAS SEASON 1

HOW TO TAKE THIS JOURNEY 7

STAGE ONE
GETTING READY FOR CHRISTMAS
The Advent Season 11

WEEK ONE
CONCERNED ABOUT TOMORROW 12

NOVEMBER 27
Blurred Vision: Where in the World is God? 13

NOVEMBER 28
Fear of Pain and Loss: Will God Let Me Suffer? 17

NOVEMBER 29
Facing the Last Enemy: When and How Will I Die? 23

NOVEMBER 30
Lingering Hope: Can I Trust the Future? 27

DECEMBER 1
Endless Waiting: How Long, O Lord? 31

DECEMBER 2
Refining Fire: When Will Righteousness Permeate the Land? 35

DECEMBER 3
Strong Deliverer: What Child is This? 39

WEEK TWO
TRUSTING GOD'S FUTURE 45

DECEMBER 4
Singing: Joy Will Return 47

DECEMBER 5
Splendor: The Glory Will Break Through 51

DECEMBER 6
Strength: Power Will Be Restored 55

DECEMBER 7
Salvation: God Will Come to the Rescue 59

DECEMBER 8
Restoration: Healing Waters Will Flow 63

DECEMBER 9
Refreshment: Thirst Will Be Quenched 67

DECEMBER 10
A Highway: The Way Will Be Found 71

WEEK THREE
PREPARING FOR CHANGE 77

DECEMBER 11
Self-doubting: The Barrier to Change 79

DECEMBER 12
Believing: The Door to Change 83

DECEMBER 13
Recognizing: Seeing Change 87

DECEMBER 14
Preparing: Getting Ourselves in Shape for Change 91

DECEMBER 15
Confessing: Starting Over 95

DECEMBER 16
Progressing: Living Life Forward 99

DECEMBER 17
Humbling: Getting Down to Earth 103

WEEK FOUR
WAITING FOR THE MIRACLE 109

DECEMBER 18
Foretelling Angel 111

DECEMBER 19
Confused and Righteous Joseph 115

DECEMBER 20
Overwhelmed Mary 121

DECEMBER 21
Right Timing 125

DECEMBER 22
Suitable Name 129

DECEMBER 23
Specific Place 133

DECEMBER 24 (CHRISTMAS EVE)
Unto Whom? 139

STAGE TWO
LIVING CHRISTMAS
Thirteen Beginning Days 144

DECEMBER 25 (CHRISTMAS DAY)
The Dawn: Living in the Brightness 146

DECEMBER 26
At Home: Living with a Larger Family 150

DECEMBER 27
In the Neighborhood: Living Next Door 154

DECEMBER 28
In the World: Living Everywhere 158

DECEMBER 29
For Everyone: Living Inclusively 162

DECEMBER 30
The Beautiful Life: Living Holy 166

DECEMBER 31 (NEW YEAR'S EVE)
Deep Gratitude: Living Thankfully 172

JANUARY 1 (NEW YEAR'S DAY)
Future Present: Living in the Hope 178

JANUARY 2
Uncommon Confidence: Living above Fear 182

JANUARY 3
Strange Confection: Living Blended Lives 186

JANUARY 4
Christlike Humility: Living without Illusion 190

JANUARY 5
Deep Joy: Living in the Surprises of God 194

JANUARY 6 (EPIPHANY)
Star Journey: Living Brightly in the Darkness 200

THE IMPORTANCE OF THE ADVENT-CHRISTMAS SEASON

(Please read this before beginning your 41-day journey.)

Christmas is about the most important breakthrough in human history. Begun in Bethlehem, it climaxed thirty years later in the broken power of sin's curse. The apostle Paul wrote of the crucifixion event as the cancellation of the condemning bond, a decisive disarmament of the principalities and powers (Colossians 2:14-15). But the *breakthrough* came at Bethlehem.

Consider all that God had to break through that first Christmas in order to bring salvation to us: Herod's awful infant pogrom, the misguided expectations of a race of vassal people who were looking for a very different kind of salvation, the low estate of a common Palestinian handmaiden who never dreamed *she* could bear the Messiah, the illiterate minds of crude shepherds who couldn't begin to articulate the Miracle into which they were about to be thrust, the literate minds of three astrologers who had intellectual skills but were far inadequate to capture the full meaning of Incarnation, and a world of darkness in which the light of salvation cradled in human flesh was incomprehensible. God had to break through all that—and more.

The Christmas message is that He succeeded. And there's more to it. Because He succeeded then, *today our lives can become breakthroughs!* If God actually became flesh, if His saving presence became available and personal to us in the Christ, then we need no longer be trapped in a prison of alienation from God. God can break through and shatter our prison walls to free us. He has found a way.

Christmas celebrates this breakthrough. In the Bethlehem story, we see the cutting edge of God's self-revealing begin to break our spiritual inertia. We see God unleashing Himself in the world. We see Him unleashing Himself in us. All of us who follow His Christ are called to be a part of Incarnation's continuing impact. The Incarnation is far more than a doctrine for our minds to work at grasping. It is a revolutionary breakthrough that wants us in its grip. Yes, we, all of us, are called to join the Bethlehem breakthrough! My hope for this book is that it will fall into the hands of people who are or may be ready for the breakthrough.

Gift Giving

This season, of course, is a time for gifting. It reminds us of two things about who we are. We are gift-givers, and we are gift-receivers. We give to one another, and we receive from one another. How and why we do this is what makes us either very human (made in God's image) or perhaps not so human. I'm sure our Lord would love to help us get better at both the giving and the receiving.

It's interesting how we approach gift-shopping differently. Keitha (my wife), who has an almost infallible sense of what a bargain is, will almost never pay a cent more than her own calculation of real value. She gets the perfect gift for someone at the best price. Our daughters Heather and Holly and our son-in-law Jack—all of them computer-savvy—get great Christmas gift deals online. As for me, well, I'm frankly at a loss. To be honest, I'm a pretty poor Yule-time shopper.

This brings me to the question of *why* we do all this shopping for Christmas gifts. Of course, it's become a habit, and habits have a way of persisting. December comes, and the remembered habit kicks in. We're expected to give gifts to close family members and some close friends and maybe a few fellow workers. It becomes such an expectation that we can feel hurt when a person who has consistently given us a Christmas gift every year doesn't come through this year. You wonder if for some reason he or she no longer likes or values you. Did you ignore or disappoint or hurt that person in some way? It may suddenly dawn on you that you forgot to give him or her a gift last year.

Why *Do* We Do It?

Christmas gift-giving can become so complicated! This is especially true when we lose sight of why we do it in the first place. Christians haven't always given gifts at Christmas. In fact, it's a fairly recent practice that developed rather late over the course of our almost two-thousand-year Christian history. It began with our worship of the Christ Child during the Christmas season— worship that called for a response in giving Him our best, as did the Magi from the East. It was not that the Christ was a god that needed to be won over, appeased or manipulated with gift offerings. There was something else to it—something entirely different. This Baby, this Jesus, this God in Human Flesh, was Himself the Gift. The Gift God gave us was Himself, and it came, not on a golden platter or in expensive gold-wrapped gift paper, but on plain straw. The greatest Gift in the humblest surroundings. Go figure.

So what do we offer this God who humbled Himself by becoming one of us and then giving Himself to us? What does this Giver-Who-Became-the-Gift desire from us? I think He wants the same as He gave us. He wants us to give ourselves to Him, and for that matter, He wants us to give ourselves to each other. In the gift economy of God, giving ourselves in love to God and giving ourselves in love to each other go hand in hand (See I John 4:7-21!).

Gifts to Those We Love

How do we give gifts to a Christ who is no longer physically present on Earth? We find Him in those we care about most and in those we meet during the day—and especially, says Jesus, in "the least of these" (Matthew 25:40). When Christians get right down to it, they are called to look for Christ in everyone and treat them as if Christ Himself were somehow there. Any gift we give to another—words, actions, tangible expressions—is a way to give ourselves to that person, similar to how Christ gives Himself to us—which is to say, graciously and with love. Or to say it even better, when we give a gift to someone else, we are also gifting Christ.

And perhaps, we can think of our receiving gifts as an expression of our receiving Christ's undeserved gifts. For followers of Jesus, the giving and receiving of gifts is not a tit-for-tat transaction. It is a touch of undeserved grace and self-giving love. Christ makes gift-receivers of us by inviting us to receive Him, the Giver, and He makes gift-givers of us by showing us how to be gracious in our giving—givers leveraging nothing for ourselves, neither approval, nor admiration, nor benefit. We give gifts at Christmas simply to say, "We care about you. We value you. We give ourselves to you." This is the sheer joy and pleasure of it.

The Gift-Giving Trinity

Jesus was not against giving gifts. In fact, He said His heavenly Father was a far better gift-giver than the best of us (Matthew 7:11; Luke 11:13). He gave the gift of His Son for our salvation (John 3:16-17). Further, He gives the gift of the Holy Spirit to those who ask Him (Luke 11:8). Of course, God gives us a seemingly infinite number of material gifts, none of them to be taken for granted, not even our daily bread, which itself deserves asking for (Matthew 6:11; Luke 11:3).

Personally, I don't think this fits in very well with the mad dash of Black Friday, where it's hard to see gratitude—only a grasping for the best deal for oneself and one's inner circle. Do we really need to have all those products or enticing ads creating our appetite for them? Typical commercials to the contrary, no one will love us more because of what we buy them. And we will love no one more, because we think the gift we gave them somehow enhances them.

Post-Christmas

During the days leading up to Christmas, we will find warm-hearted stories on the television or the internet. They will portray acts of compassion and self-giving. And as Christmas nears, some of them may be more specifically associated with the Christian gospel and the birth of Jesus. As soon as Christmas has passed, however, we will be showered with the after-Christmas sales we won't want to miss. These sales will keep the adrenalin flowing and the mounting exhaustion or even depression at bay. We will wonder if we missed something important—important to our faith, important to our spirits, important to our Lord? Was Christmas only the passing fancy of another year's end? Can Christmas live on past Christmas?

These Meditations

The aim of this book is twofold. To begin with, it will help you prepare for Christmas, as this preparation is the purpose of the Advent season. In addition, it will help you to live Christmas, which is the purpose of the season beginning with Christmas Day. This is a book of meditations prayed and prepared for the purpose of opening your heart and your faith to a breakthrough. It uses reflection on Scripture to help you explore the preparation and drama of God's Incarnation in the Man Jesus and then to see how you can actually enter that story and live it day by day. In doing so, it will hopefully help you see how the real meaning of Christmas is being confiscated so often by other messages that have at best diluted, and at worst destroyed, the real gifts of this season.

The preparatory *Advent meditations* span four complete weeks. They cover a wide range of matters for us to address personally in preparation for receiving the gift of the Christ in fresh ways. Week One addresses some of the deep concerns we have about the future, concerns we can then bring to God. Week Two is a meditation on a detailed prophecy of restoration in Isaiah, a prophecy Christians believe began to be fulfilled with the coming of Christ and will be completely fulfilled at His return. Week Three takes us through the process of the change required if we are to be prepared for receiving Jesus. And Week Four takes us through the story of surprises and miracles leading up to the birth of Jesus. We hope these Advent meditations will challenge your thinking and more importantly your heart. We hope they will ready you for a new coming of Christ into your life.

The *Christmas meditations* span thirteen days: Christmas Day and the twelve days following. All of the meditations in this section deal with what it means to *live* Christmas. They go beyond the feel-good aspects of our Christmas celebrations. They focus instead on the real purpose of Christ's coming. What is now possible in light of the Incarnation? How does this miraculous event affect our attitudes, our day-to-day lives and how we live them? How are we changed, because God is now with us, one of us, friend of us, expander of us, leader of us, lover of us? And where are our lives now heading? These are essential questions to be answered by any follower of Jesus. May these meditations help you begin to find the answers.

HOW TO TAKE THIS JOURNEY

(Also read this before starting the meditations)

There are basically three parts to each meditation. The first is a Scripture passage or group of passages which relate in some way to the reading that follows. I suggest that the passage(s) be read very carefully and prayerfully. You may want to meditate for a few minutes on something that particularly strikes you in the reading. The second is the written meditation itself, which is designed to stimulate your thinking and guide your reflection in a direction related to the Scripture passage. There may be other Scripture verses or passages referenced in the course of a meditation, which you will want to consult. The third part is a concluding prayer shaped by the Scripture and the meditation. In each individual case, you may find the prayer helpful, add to it, or simply pray your own prayer.

It is important that this time of meditation takes place in a controlled setting where interruptions are less likely to distract you. For many, that time would be in the early morning. For others for whom private space is next to impossible at that time of day, another time in the day when it's possible to be alone will be chosen.

Although the meditations are designed for one's private devotions, it may be desirable for a very small group—for example, a married couple—to do the meditations together, followed by a time of sharing. Two to four people could actually do them together through a scheduled conference call each day. Perhaps a group of people who are doing the meditations alone could meet or do a conference call once a week to share what that week's journey has meant to them and to pray together for each other. Please use the meditations as flexibly as you need to!

A Little More Information about Advent, Christmas and Epiphany for Those Who Are Interested:

It is helpful to know why the Christian Church decided to create an Advent season leading up to the Christmas season. Centuries ago, the Church realized that spiritual preparation was necessary for followers of Jesus to be able to grasp the deep significance of the Incarnation in a way that empowered them to embody it in their lives. Otherwise, Christmas Day would simply be one high holy day preceded and followed by many low unholy days. It would make little real difference in their lives. The season of Advent (meaning 'coming,' referring to the coming of Christ into the world) was established to help Christians ready their hearts and lives for a new birthing of Christ in them. The Twelve Days of Christmas (beginning with Christmas Day) was established to continue the celebration of Christmas and stir devotion to the Christ Child in such a way as to make a positive difference in a Christian's living.

This book of meditations follows a similar path, with only one adjustment made in order for the reader to be able to use it during the Advent-Christmas season of *any* year: It is organized by specific dates in our yearly calendar. Giving four full weeks for the Advent season, it begins on November 27, allowing for twenty-eight days of preparation, the last day being Christmas Eve. This is a little earlier than the Advent season begins in the traditional Church calendar (the first of four Sundays before

Christmas, regardless of the actual calendar date). Considering that Christmas advertising begins before Thanksgiving, and Christmas sales begin the day after Thanksgiving, perhaps the sooner we start the Advent journey, the better! (Incidently, for the early Celtic Church in the British Isles, Advent began on November 16!)

Christmas Day (December 25) then becomes the first of thirteen days to explore what it means to *live* Christmas. It concludes with Epiphany (January 6) which is the thirteenth day added to the traditional twelve days of Christmas. Epiphany is the celebration of Christ as the Light that has come into this darkened world, capped by the invitation for us to follow the Light by actually living in the light.

"Therefore, brothers and sisters, you must be patient as you wait for the coming of the Lord" (James 5:7a).

STAGE ONE

GETTING READY FOR CHRISTMAS
The Advent Season

An Advent Prayer
Lord, it's a long way from Thanksgiving to Christmas,
a long time to listen to the incessant assault of Christmas songs
and yes, even carols blaring on the radio and TV waves
from loudspeakers in malls reworking a Christian festival
into a sentimental backdrop for commerce,
and even in church gatherings too impatient for some
expected Christmas magic,
too unaware and impenitent to be ready for
anything startling when the time is ripe.
Lord, give me Advent before I presume to be in shape for Christmas,
space for my longing, waiting, preparing for Christ,
a season to see the darkness around me, and within me,
an opportunity to open my life to a new spiritual invasion
offending my convenient blindness, opening my heart to judgment,
so that grace can come and Christ be born.
Then, Lord, I may be ready for Christmas, ready for miracles,
transformation, hope,
instead of the wearing down brought on by overexposure,
by desperately grabbing too much, too soon, too quickly,
what can only be known by a clearer vision, a humble patience,
a painful purification of the soul to prepare me for the promise of
Christ.
Come, Lord Jesus, when I'm ready to confront what is around me,
and within me—and not before. Amen

WEEK ONE

CONCERNED ABOUT TOMORROW

NOVEMBER 27

Blurred Vision: Where in the World is God?

Scripture—Matthew 11:2-6

The world is living in a fog of uncertainty. Confidence about the future is at an all-time low. It wasn't that long ago that most people believed in a caring God who could be relied upon to show us the way to tomorrow. They were confident about the future. Belief in such a God, however, has been declining.

It is not hard to see one of the major reasons: Christians. Our witness has lost so much credibility. Consider some of the reasons: the much publicized scandals of Christian leaders; smug churches that turn off sincere seekers; a settled Christianity without passion; doctrinal positions too aligned with political party agendas; rampant hypocrisy; lack of empathy for the poor and marginalized (the very people Jesus spent the great majority of His time with). The problem, dear Christian reader, is with us—those who consider themselves the people of God. We have helped to create the fog of uncertainty. Our Christian living is insufficiently convincing.

Another development has contributed to the fog. The advances of science have placed religious faith on the back burner or completely off the table of many people's world views. Exploration of endless galaxies has caused many to question that a Creator of this infinity would be so absorbed by this one planet (Earth) and its inhabitants. Creation is now understood, says James Carroll, " … as the infinitely expanding cosmos, rushing madly away from an unknown center, with humanity ever more marginal, insignificant, and puny" (*Christ Actually*, pp. 42-43). So how do we Christians think we can speak with convincing authority from our little place in this ever-expanding space?

Years ago, I had a friend who gradually moved from Christian faith to agnosticism. He had a brilliant mind which he trusted explicitly. If the existence of something, including God, could not be proven by scientific evidence, he would not allow himself to believe it. In a couple of long conversations with him by email before he passed away, I learned that he still had a deep emotional attachment to Salvation Army brass band music and to certain Christian pieces in the classical repertoire, and he listened to them frequently. They would often move him to tears. This made me wonder if he had become a person with two sides that he could no longer integrate. He seemed to keep his intellectual side and his feeling side separate. Since one cannot truly embrace Christian faith with the mind alone, he could not let himself be a Christian. Disciples of Jesus do not check their minds at the doors of their Christianity, but they do recognize the limitations of rational thinking, which can take us only so far before it meets mystery. Mystery is not fantasy; it is reality beyond the rational. Scientists come up against it all the time. It is the thing they can't explain but can only know in a different way.

I think my friend's division within himself characterizes many people in our day. It is more difficult for them to see God at work in the world and easier to see or imagine contradictions that blur such vision. John the Baptist is well known as the forerunner of Jesus, as he prepared the way for Jesus' messianic debut and even went so far as to encourage his own followers to give their allegiance to Jesus. After John was arrested and awaited trial, he began to puzzle over Jesus. He who was so certain that Jesus was the

Messiah sent by God now seemed to be less certain. Was doubt beginning to creep into his mind? He might have been asking, *Is there a reason some followers of Jesus are beginning to fall away? Where is the Messiah who, with winnowing fork in hand will clear His threshing floor and gather His wheat into the granary, but burn the chaff with unquenchable fire* (Matthew 3:12)? John had not predicted a Messiah of such patience, tolerance, gentleness, empathy and compassion as people have seen in Jesus. At the very least, the Baptizer wanted further confirmation from Jesus. He instructed one of his disciples to go to Jesus and ask, "Are you the one who is to come, or should we look for another?"

John was trying to figure it all out. He clearly expected a more forceful Messiah who would get things done right away—as did most of the Jews of that day. Why wasn't Jesus making things happen? Where was the Kingdom He was supposed to be ushering in? Jesus' answer to John's messenger was simply this: *The Kingdom of God came when I came. It's hidden within us* (Luke 17:21). *I'm living it now. Go report to John what you hear and see. The blind now see. The cripples walk. Those with skin diseases are cleansed. The deaf hear. The dead are raised up. The poor have the good news proclaimed to them. This is the Kingdom breaking through in the way that will radically change lives and last forever. Happy (blessed) are those who don't stumble and fall, because I'm not ushering in the Kingdom of God they expect or thought they wanted.*

Even John the Baptist (whose prophetic integrity and effectiveness Jesus goes on to praise) didn't yet fully grasp the evidence for the new Kingdom's presence and power. So we should not be embarrassed about our own defective hearing and blurred vision of how God is at work in the world. We may well not be hearing or seeing what is really there. We may be listening to some wrong signals or only hearing selectively. We may be looking in some of the wrong places or not seeing what is really before us.

At the beginning of this Advent season, Jesus invites us to hear and see things differently. He calls us to join Him on a journey, every turn of which reveals something new or different about God and His ways. You may have missed a turn or two, blurring your vision of how He is at work in the world and in your own life. Let your Advent journey begin now—with your willingness to better see God's Kingdom and the ways He is at work in the world where He has placed you.

Prayer

Dear Lord, I confess that I am sometimes blinded by my fears, my selfishness, my insecurities and my false hopes. Take from my sight the blurring barrier of my presumption and replace it with the clarity of a humble mind and a purified heart—so that I can begin to see with clearer vision how You are present in the world and how I am called to live my life in Your presence here. I pray this through Jesus Emmanuel, 'God with us.' Amen.

NOVEMBER 28

Fear of Pain and Loss: Will God Let Me Suffer?

Scripture—I Peter 1:6-7; 3:13-17

Some Christians—and probably all of us at times—have believed or wished that if we do this or that certain thing to please the Almighty, or if we pray enough, God will not allow us to suffer serious pain or loss. Keitha and I do pray and study our Bible. But suffering and loss still invade our lives. To illustrate, here's what happened fairly recently over the course of a year:

> Two of Keitha's brothers suffered debilitating strokes. Keitha fell twice, breaking an upper arm the first time and both her wrists the second. My sister received a diagnosis of cancer and underwent both surgery and radiation. Her housemate was the victim of a freak car accident, breaking her pelvis. A very close friend died suddenly from a fall. A beloved uncle died. A spiritual mother to us passed away. Friends found themselves in a crisis they couldn't have imagined. On top of it all, our country was plagued by a maelstrom of scandal and government dysfunction—enough to send anyone into a state of depression.

Did someone not pray enough or spend sufficient time in the Word? Why did God not give us a protective shield? Does He not care about those who love and serve Him?

During the Great Depression, Josephine W. Johnson wrote a novel about a family who had to flee their father's failed business in the city to an old farm under mortgage. Each year, as the drought worsened, the farm was unable to produce a sufficient harvest. Matching the effects of the damaging drought, relationships within the family also suffered and declined. The eldest of the daughters became emotionally unhinged and committed suicide. Not long afterward, the mother died from the effects of burns received when the family fought a wildfire. She, a devout Christian, had been the family's stability. The middle daughter, Marget, the narrator of the novel, described the tragic effect her mother's death had on her:

> Once I thought there were words for all things except love and intolerable beauty. Now I know that there is a third thing beyond expression—the sense of loss. There are no words for death. … I could not pretend or hope any longer, or believe blindly in any goodness. It was all gone. Faith swept away like a small mound of grass, and nothing to wait or live for any longer. God was only a name, and it was [Mother's] life that had been the meaning of that name. Now there was nothing left (*Now in November*, pp. 223-224).

It is very hard for some to believe in a God who allows us to suffer such pain and loss.

Life is fragile for all of us. Tragedy can strike at any time. A shooter can walk into a school, a church, a concert and snuff out innocent lives indiscriminately. A sudden heart attack or stroke can do the same. Cancer can attack a healthy body and bring early death. Innocents get murdered in crossfires. Lovers of God are not protected from tragedy.

I often think of my grandfather Walter Needham who fought in the British Army during WWI. One day, his company was outnumbered and overrun by a much larger German unit, killing all but a few in Walter's company. Walter himself had multiple wounds and became a prisoner of war in a camp where little medical attention was given. Seen as incurable, he was transported to the Swiss Red Cross who over time miraculously saved his life. Reunited with his wife and infant son (my father), he immigrated later to America where he served as a Salvation Army officer, primarily in the Adult Rehabilitation ministry. He retired early because of deteriorating health. During his last years, delayed PTSD emerged, and he began reliving the horrors of the war. He had survived the war, but the brokenness, long hidden, had returned.

We all carry with us our brokenness and pain. Should we think about such things during the Advent season when bells are ringing, bands are playing carols, and glittering decorations abound? Thinking about loss seems to go against the spirit of the season. Speaking of pain and suffering surely interferes with the cascade of uplifting messages and the eager anticipations of what we so long for. Or is the reason so many get depressed during this season because they suppress the pain in their lives, and the hidden pain then feeds on them.

The Advent season was never intended as a feel-good season, though many churches treat it as such by making December a month-long celebration of the gift of the Christ Child. The truth is that we are not in any state to receive this Gift of all gifts without preparing ourselves. Without owning our brokenness and asking for healing. Without knowing our pain and asking for strength to bear it. Without confessing our emptiness and asking for our lives to be filled with the miracle that began with this Child. And then to realize that the suffering doesn't end, as Peter says above, and as Paul is told by Ananias (Acts 9:13-17). We should not think of the Christ Child without knowing, as Simeon prophesied, that He would face opposition and come to a terrible death that would pierce His mother's heart (Luke 2:33-35).

As a captured German soldier in WWII, Jürgen Moltmann was imprisoned in a wretched prisoner-of-war camp in Belgium. The German Reich had collapsed, and the cruel inhumanity of the German government had been exposed. Jürgen's hometown, Hamburg, lay in ruins. He felt the same about his own life. The hopes of his youth had died; he felt abandoned by God and humans alike:

> One day an American chaplain put a Bible into his hands, and he began to read it. He was especially drawn to the story of Jesus' suffering. As he recounted later, "When I came to Jesus' death cry, I knew: This is the one who understands you and is beside you when everyone else abandons you. 'My God, why have you forsaken me?' ... I began to understand the suffering, assailed and God-forsaken Jesus, because I felt he understood me. And I began to understand that this Jesus is the divine Brother in our distress" (E.J. Dionne Jr., "God, as We Hadn't Seen Him," Atlanta Journal-Constitution, Dec. 25, 2003).

Jürgen Moltmann became a follower of Jesus and a theologian best known for his writings about the Christian message of hope. As we make this Advent journey to the Child in the manger, let us not only embrace the beautiful miracle of this Child who is Emmanuel—God now present with us. Let us also embrace the way He showed us to live, the way of the Cross through our pain and our losses, with the joy within us and before us of which no person or circumstance can rob us.

Prayer

Dear Lord, as You suffered through pain and loss, accepting it as part of Your calling, help me to do the same. In giving You full claim on my heart, I also give You full claim on my life. I ask You to remove what is of insufficient worth, and I ask You for grace to endure unanticipated misfortune, none of which will separate me from Your love. I pray in Your name, who suffered a cruel but saving death for me. Amen.

NOVEMBER 29

Facing the Last Enemy: When and How Will I Die?

Scripture—Romans 6:5; II Corinthians 4:10-18

James Boswell, who enjoyed questioning his mentor Samuel Johnson, once asked Johnson if the fear of death was natural to humans. "So much so," answered Johnson, "that the whole of life is but keeping away the thoughts of it." It's not as hard to do that when we're young, and death seems so far off. As we grow older, however, we become increasingly aware that death is a reality that is actually going to come to us, probably sooner than later. We think about it more, and as we grow weak with age, perhaps see it as almost a friend. More and more, our bodies seem like fragile drinking glasses that have been used often and will inevitably break.

Death is a reality we can't control. Short of a planned and executed suicide, death comes on its own timetable. Most of us have some sense of a span of life we think we can or have a right to expect. And then a precious small child dies of a disease or from want, a beloved teenage son is killed by a car, a wife and mother dies of cancer in her thirties, or a spiritual leader of many souls dies of a heart attack in his early forties. It throws us for a loop, maybe even drives us to despair. Why does God allow this? Why, of all people, these people? And why must genuinely good people sometimes have to suffer long, painful and debilitating illnesses, until finally, death comes as a sweet relief? And why, on the other hand, does this or that scoundrel live comfortably into his nineties?

These are questions for which we have no answers. That doesn't stop some of us from coming up with "explanations" that don't really help. *God loved this man so much that He wanted him to be with Him sooner.* (Is God that selfish?) *This woman, even though young, had completed her ministry on Earth, so God took her.* (You mean she couldn't possibly have been of any more help to anyone had she lived longer?) Such facile rationalizations to justify God may temporarily meet our need to bring some kind of meaning or order to the situation, but it will bring no long-term, settled comfort to those most bereaved. Furthermore, does God actually need us to justify Him?

When the time will come for us to die, there will probably be more we would have liked to have done before leaving this earth. Moses would have liked to have entered the promised land after forty years of leading his fellow escaped slaves through thick and thin, but he had to settle for a glance at a distance. A young mother would have liked to have seen her children grow up; a middle-aged mother would have loved to have seen her first grandchild. Parents would have loved to have seen their promising daughter find success in the political career she had begun to pursue. Soldiers killed in the American Revolutionary War would have liked to have enjoyed the benefits of a free nation for which they had sacrificed their lives. Death robs so many people of things they would have loved to have known or experiences they would have loved to have had. Perhaps this is why some who are dying refuse to accept that they are being denied what they saw as the next phases of their earthly lives.

In the world in which and to which the New Testament was written, there was a pervasive belief in fatalism: Whatever will be, will be. You can't change your fate. If doom is written in your stars, there's nothing you can do about it. The apostle Paul spoke to this world of a rescue: Christ stared death in the face for all of us, in the knowledge that He was to be " ... the first crop of the harvest of those who have died"—He, the resurrection and the life for those who believe with their hearts and their lives. Death is the last enemy to be defeated (I Cor. 15:1-28). For us, said Dietrich Bonhoeffer, "Death is the supreme festival on the road to freedom."

We are not given control over when or how we die. Christ, the One in whom our confidence and hope lies, gives us the Gift of His life. Which is to say, we are given *Him*. He *is* life eternal. He is the Way, the Truth, and the Life—or as James Moffatt translates, "the true and living Way." Whatever the circumstances of our deaths, we will face them with Him who is the resurrection and the life. He who taught us how to begin living eternal life now brings us to its fulfillment.

Who is prepared for this? Who is ready to separate himself from this life for the life to come? Two lines from a Robert Frost poem give us a clue. Frost speaks of "The many deaths one must have died/ Before he came to meet his own" ("The Wind and the Rain," *The Poetry of Robert Frost*, p. 336). Jesus calls us to die to ourselves again and again in order to discover our true selves and to follow Him (Matthew 16:24-25; Mark 8:34-35; Luke 9:23-24). Death begins when we come to faith and start shedding our false selves. Those most prepared for their earthly deaths are those who have let die their pretensions and let live their true selves in the image of God.

Henry Francis Lyte was a beloved pastor, a gifted preacher and a prolific hymn writer in England. Because of ill health, he was forced to leave his pulpit for periods of time. Finally, he did not have the physical strength to continue his ministry. It was necessary for him to retire. With great difficulty, he preached his last sermon to a congregation whose hearts were full with the realization that this would probably be the last time they would hear their pastor preach. That afternoon, after the service, Henry walked out along the shore to watch the sun at its setting in a glory of crimson and gold. Returning home, he shut himself in his study and wrote the last of his hymns, "Abide with Me." It closed with these lines:

I fear no foe with Thee at hand to bless; Ills have no weight and tears no bitterness. Where is death's sting? Where, grave, thy victory? I triumph still, if Thou abide with me! (*The Song Book of The Salvation Army*, #529)

With such faith, such freedom from fear, we can face the last enemy, no matter when death comes or how it comes.

Prayer

Dear God, as I prepare myself this season for the coming of Your Son into our world, teach me not only to live life fully as He did, but also to face death with acceptance as He did. By your grace, motivate me to die daily to those things not worth having or doing, to the indulgences and diversions that distract my discipleship, and to the self-serving drives that diminish my soul. And then, dear Lord, when my earthly death comes, no matter how it comes to me, by Your grace walk with me hand in hand as I cross over to the joy of Your eternal presence and love. I pray this in the name of Your Son who tasted death for me. Amen.

NOVEMBER 30

Lingering Hope: Can I Trust the Future?

Scripture—Psalm 126; Luke 21:25-33

We humans tend to be optimistic—until we turn pessimistic. We go through cycles, sometimes within the same day. On an emotional level, optimism is a feeling that things are going to get better; pessimism a feeling that the future does not look good. Which emotion one has can relate to a number of factors: high or low self-esteem, upbringing, the influence of powerful people in one's life. On a more objective level, both optimism and pessimism can be based on observable evidence. You see a definite trend; you see the makings of a better or a worse future.

Someone has said that the greatest difference between people is what they anticipate. You've probably heard this ditty before:

Two men looked out of prison bars
The one saw mud, the other stars.

(Dale Carnegie, *How to Stop Worrying and Start Living*)

What you anticipate tells you what your life is about. It suggests what your vision of tomorrow is. If your life is committed to that vision and you are working toward it, you are revealing who you are, no matter what your present circumstances. Our hope defines us.

Advent is the season of anticipation. Popular songs are full of it, from the nostalgia of "I'm Dreaming of a White Christmas" to the longing for family in "I'll Be Home for Christmas." Oddly, some adults think the possibility of a really bad Christmas can be used to get children to be on their best behavior during the season. It comes in the words of a rather cruel Christmas song we're all familiar with: "You better watch out/You better not cry/You better not pout/I'm telling you why: Santa Claus is comin' to town!" Get in shape, kids, or you won't get the goodies! (Don't let the cute tune fool you. Say it to yourself in the gruff voice of a grinch.)

This longing for a happy Christmas may be one expression of our greater longing for a better future. By the time Jesus was born, the Jewish people had for centuries been longing for deliverance from their oppressors. Their psalmists cried out for this deliverance in agonizing poetry; their prophets saw it in visions of a God-anointed savior who would proclaim and grant the deliverance. Christians believe that Jesus, the saving Messiah, did indeed come—freeing those who received Him, not from external oppressors but from the oppression of their own sinful hearts, their compromised lives, their abuse of each other.

The psalmist declares God's goodness to His people in the past and then asks for a similar future in which what they have sown in tears becomes an abundant harvest. He hopes God will come through for His people as He has done in the past. In another psalm, the writer David isn't so sure (Psalm 22:1-5): "My, God! My God! why have you left me all alone?" These very words were repeated by Jesus Himself on the cross. He was not simply quoting from the psalm for effect or to state some doctrinal principle about God the Father, who was disgusted by the enormity of sin Jesus had taken on Himself, turning His face and His heart away from His beloved Son. Jesus the Man was honestly crying out as a result of the pain of His forsakenness.

In the gross uncertainty of the days in which we are living, as the world seems to be falling apart, many people wonder if God has abandoned us. When terrible things happen to good or innocent people, we wonder where hope has gone. We sometimes wonder if God is there for us. And then we hear the cry of dereliction from the cross, and we realize that Jesus experienced this too. And He cried out His feeling of utter forsakenness by God. He may be giving us permission to do the same. To be honest in our times of despair. To be upfront about our times of feeling God's absence.

What does it mean to believe that God is there for us if we cannot honestly confess or cry when we don't *feel* it is so. Should we pretend piety to cover honest uncertainty? The psalmist, and Jesus Himself, knew God would be there for them, but they didn't mince their words when He seemed so far away. So many things are happening these days to make people wonder if the future can be trusted. So many questions unanswered. So many hopes dashed.

Hope, however, still hangs around. And we, the people of God, still hold it, or maybe it holds us. We are like Moses when he was leading a multitude of slaves to a Promised Land. They took many wrong turns, lost their faith time and again, almost turned back. It took them forty years to get there. In the face of his own doubt and the doubts of his fellow travelers, Moses kept saying one word: *remember*. Remember how God carried you just as a parent carries a child (Deuteronomy 1:310). Remember how He has seen you through our times of helplessness and threat.

This Advent season is about hope for the future. We followers of Jesus stand alongside the children of Israel with plenty of reasons sometimes to feel God's absence, but with more reasons to believe His seeming withdrawal is temporary, and He will be there tomorrow. We stand alongside Jesus when He says in the passage from Luke that "Heaven and Earth will pass away, but my words will certainly not pass away." We stand alongside our resurrected Lord when He assures His disciples He will be with them " ... every day until the end of this present age" (Matthew 28:20b)—even when it doesn't seem so.

This Advent season, let hope capture you. Let Christ, the One who disarmed the principalities and powers, be your hope (Colossians 2:15). When you come to the Christ Child this Christmas Eve, know that in this manger lies the hope of the world. Come prepared to give yourself to Him again, perhaps in a new way. Indeed, you are part of the hope.

Prayer

God of hope, open my eyes, my heart, my thinking, my life, to the miracle of Your actual presence in the world. Help me to own the miracle even though some days, I do not feel it or see it. Especially on those days, give me the courage to risk living the hope, as did Jesus at great cost and at unlimited benefit to the world. I pray this in His name and for His glory. Amen.

December 1

Endless Waiting: How Long, O Lord?

Scripture—James 5:7-10

We live in a world of spoiled children. People want instantaneous information on the internet, immediate investment returns, overnight fortunes, fast foods, painless cures and quick fixes. We are gratifying ourselves to death. It seems the only way we can grasp providence is to make it into something God does for us right away. Catering to spoiled Christians, an ample supply of God-give-it-to-me-now hucksters have appeared on the Church scene to feed the incessant craving.

Providence, however, is not God spoiling us every day. It is the promise of eternity. The children of His providence know how to wait, and the truly wonderful things in life happen to those who are willing to live by God's timing and trust His future. There are indeed times of deep fulfillment on our Christian journey, moments when everything seems to come together perfectly, spiritual peaks, times when the joy that nothing can rob us of is in full bloom. These are previews— "foretastes of glory divine"—and we treasure these moments and the memory of them. They are hints of our future in Christ.

But that future is not spelled out for us in detail. It is a future God will bring to pass in His own way. Although we would like to figure it out to the letter, that is not going to happen. Providence is not the discovery of a detailed plan; it is the trustworthiness of a gracious Person. No matter what the immediate circumstances seem to be saying about their future prospects, the people of God trust the providence of God.

Advent is about the future. Our future, yes, but more importantly, God's future. As the Jews waited centuries for God to release them from bondage, so we wait for the full realization of the Kingdom of God that Jesus launched almost two thousand years ago.

Two thousand years ago! So what's the delay now? Sometimes, we get frustrated with all the waiting. Are we supposed to spend the rest of our lives on Earth waiting? Well, yes, we probably will but with eager anticipation—and with plenty to do.

Perhaps we could call this *active waiting*. It is waiting, because it will be God Himself who brings His Kingdom to fulfillment, not us. It is active, because we do not sit around passively waiting for God to take care of everything in the world that needs fixing. We have been given some explicit instructions on how to wait as followers of Jesus. For starters, take a look at Jesus' Sermon on the Mount recorded in Matthew, chapters 5-7. Take a look at the entire New Testament! It's all about how we wait actively. We start *now*, by the grace of God, to live by the law of love that is the core of the Kingdom of God that Jesus gave us. Love God (Matthew 22:37; Mark 12:30, 33a; Luke 10:27). Love your fellow Christians (John 13:34-35; 15:12, 17). Love your neighbors (Matthew 19:19; 22:39; Mark 12:31; Luke 10:27b). Love your enemies (Matthew 5:44; Luke 6:27, 35). Our hands are not tied behind our backs, our hearts are not blocked. Jesus has released us to live God's future *now*! Those are our marching orders!

> Speed the Cross through all the nations,
> Speed the victories of love,
> Preach the gospel of redemption

Wheresoever men [and women] may move;
Make the future in the present,
Strong of heart, toil on and sing.

(Hymn writer Walter J. Mathams)

Yes, make the future in the present! *Sing!*

Indeed, Advent is a season for singing! We sing our praise. We sing our songs of hope. We sing of God in human flesh. We sing of our Lord. We sing our love. We sing our gratitude. We sing our commitment to Jesus and the mission of His life. It's music, not drudgery. It's overflowing song, not dead ritual. And as we wait for the fullness of God's Kingdom to come, we sing our longing from deep within.

We sing while we actively wait. We sing while we're down. We sing when we're happy. We sing while we work for our Master from the dawn to setting sun. We sing when we're together and when we're alone. As a community of faith, we sing in the plural, and in our own personal love relationship with the Lord, we sing our love in the singular.

We listen to God singing His love song to us—singing His longing for us to follow His Son, Jesus, and receive His Holy Spirit. He's wooing us to our calling. He wants us to sing to Him with our lives, to join with the psalmist and say, "I will sing to the Lord all my life; I will sing praise to my God as long as I live" (Psalm 104:33).

As you wait this Advent season, consider the song God is calling you to sing. When you long for Christ's liberating presence, sing "Come, Thou long expected Jesus/Born to set Thy people free." When you feel exiled, sing "O come, o come Emmanuel/And ransom captive Israel." When you're in need of guidance, sing "So, most gracious Lord, may we/Evermore be led to Thee." In times of fullness, sing "Dear desire of every nation,/Joy of every longing heart." In times of emptiness sing your longing: "O come to us, abide with us,/Our Lord Emmanuel."

Prayer

Lord, give me patience in my waiting for Your Kingdom—not a patience that does nothing, but rather a patient pursuit to seek and find You in the world in which I live. A patience to hear past the noises and pressures around me and within me, hear Your still small voice above the clamor, so that I can seek to obey. A patience to see You in the world where You've placed me, especially in "the least of these," so that I can do my best to imitate You. Help me to live humbly in the knowledge that all miracles are from You, none from me, all of them pointing to Your Kingdom that is on its way. I pray this through Him who brought the Kingdom to us and will be its fulfillment. Amen.

DECEMBER 2

REFINING FIRE: WHEN WILL RIGHTEOUSNESS PERMEATE THE LAND?

Scripture—Malachi 2:17-3:6

At the time of this writing, America seems to be bathed in a vitriol of indecency and hatred. People are more polarized than ever, more dismissive of those who don't agree with them, more likely to overlook the deplorable acts of those with whom they agree politically. The atmosphere is so poisoned with this ugliness that more and more people are looking for some model of decency and kindness. This search may account for the highly unusual success of two documentaries the year of this writing. Documentaries don't usually draw large theater crowds, but these two documentaries have. They are documentaries about two enormously kind and decent people: Fred Rogers (*Won't You Be My Neighbor?*) and Ruth Bader Ginsburg (*RBG*). You may not like Rogers' excessive niceness (although it sure does connect with children) or Ginsburg's political leanings, but all of us can appreciate their decency and kindness. I think this may be one reason people are flocking to hear the life stories and realize the moral influence of these two extraordinary people, as if bathing in pure spring water.

In the Scripture passage above, God is also disgusted with how people are treating one another. They commit adultery, lie to each other, cheat workers out of their wages, oppress helpless widows and orphans, do not welcome migrants and do not revere the Lord Himself (3:5). Sound familiar? What is worse is that they say that because they are getting away with these sins, God is obviously not concerned, and He even delights in these evils (2:17).

On the contrary, the Lord is disgusted with this disobedience, this violation of His covenant with them—as if the covenant were a tree under whose shade they were protected from the consequences of their actions. He is ready to take decisive action:

> Look, I'm sending my messenger who will clear the path before me; suddenly the Lord whom you are seeking will come to His temple. The messenger of the covenant in whom you take delight is coming, says the Lord of heavenly forces [hosts] (3:1).

Whatever the identity of this messenger—in Hebrew, Malachi means "messenger"—He would be like a refiner's fire to purify metal or a cleaner's soap to wash away impurities (3:2b). The refining would begin with the spiritual leaders (3:3b) and then spread throughout the community. The priests were not to pretend that they alone were capable of the cleansing. On the contrary, their cleansing would be a signal for widespread cleansing—an invitation to renewal for everyone. God is here conceived as a King and the temple as His palace. He cannot come until His house is set in order. His messenger will straighten out the abuses and will restore worship offered to God with dignity and sincerity of heart (2:6). When this happens, God will right the injustices toward others and the disdain toward Him, described in 3:5.

Whoever this messenger was to be at that time, we Christians also will, of course, hear these words as an anticipation of Christ's coming in Jesus of Nazareth. The apostle Paul speaks of the outcome of Christ's rescue mission as " … cleans[ing] a special people for himself who are eager to do good actions" (Titus 2:14). An accounting will come for those who hide their disobedience and compromise behind the symbols, rituals and practices of Christian faith. Confession of sin will be called for. Purification will be needed.

We should not miss the fact that the Levites, the spiritual leaders of Malachi's day, are the initial targets for cleansing (3:3ab). For us Salvationists, this means Army leaders (international, territorial, divisional, corps) will first be purified, and if they will not, new leaders must emerge who will. Revival needs leaders who go first, and sometimes those leaders are not the ones in official positions but new leaders who emerge, like a new David described in Ezekiel 34:23.

For Malachi, only those who undergo a spiritual and moral cleansing are in a position to offer "a righteous sacrifice" (3:3c)—or as Paul said it, " … to present [their] bodies as a living sacrifice that is holy and pleasing to God" (Romans 12:1b). We call this righteousness. In the Bible, righteousness is measured in relationships. Humans are relational beings. Their true humanness is found in their relationship with God and each other. Righteousness is expressed in these relationships. It is not some "thing," some possession, some permanent mark we carry around with us. It is something we do in a relationship. I am righteous toward God when my love toward Him takes the form of willing obedience. I am righteous toward a fellow Christian when I treat him or her as a brother or sister in Christ. I am righteous toward someone who considers himself my enemy when I love him anyway—and show it. In every relationship of our lives, Christ is calling us to a specific righteousness He calls for in that relationship. Through

His sacrifice and death, and with the Holy Spirit's refining and guidance, we are empowered to live righteously in all our relationships. We, in fact, actually "become the righteousness of God" (II Corinthians 5:21), "filled with the fruit of righteousness" (Philippians 1:11).

At a time when indecency and injustice seem to dominate the affairs of this world, we may well worry about what the future has in store. It is precisely in *this* situation that Christ calls us to sanctify ourselves for a courageous righteousness rather than a cowardly isolation. We are His Advent people. Knowing that one day His Kingdom will come in fullness, our lives are spent in preparing the way. He calls us to act like credible Kingdom-of-God citizens, committing our way to the Lord, as the psalmist puts it, and trusting in Him to do this:

> He will make your righteousness shine like the dawn,
> the justice of your cause like the noonday sun (Psalm 37:5-6).

Prayer

Righteous God, please empower me to live righteously in all my relationships, not as a holier-than-thou show-off—rather, in authentic humility. Save me from the sham of a loveless righteousness. Help me to remember that acts of true righteousness are acts of genuine, godly love. I confess that I'm incapable of such love on my own, so I ask that You fill me with Your Holy Spirit, sanctify my heart with Your love, and give me the courage to stand up against any action or policy that exploits or demeans others. I ask these things in the name of my Lord Jesus Christ, who put His life on the line for me and for everyone else. Amen.

DECEMBER 3

STRONG DELIVERER: WHAT CHILD IS THIS?

Scripture—Isaiah 9:1-7

The eighth chapter of Isaiah sets the stage for the Scripture above. According to Isaiah, Assyria will be God's instrument to humble disobedient Israel and Judah. Nevertheless, they can look for signs of hope, not from mediums and spiritists who "will never see the dawn," but from a God who will keep His covenant. Otherwise, "… they will see only distress and darkness."

In the ninth chapter, however, we enter a world flooded with light:

> Nonetheless, those who were in distress won't be exhausted
> …. The people walking in darkness have seen a great light.
> On those living in a pitch-dark land, light has dawned.

Advent begins with the promise of light, the best possible news in the world of darkness. Where will the light come from? From what blazing meteor of a Messiah? From what monarch lighting up the landscape with the energy of his massive political force? The answer comes as a shocker:

> A Child is born to us, a Son is given to us, and authority will be on His shoulders (italics added).

The light of our salvation comes from a Child! As Rembrandt and many other Nativity painters show it, the only real light in the dark night of our sin comes from the manger. From this Child comes the light the darkness cannot extinguish, and those who welcome and receive this Light-Child and believe in His name become God's own children (John 1:12). The apostle Paul says the light reaches into our hearts, the center of our being, and gives us "… the light of the knowledge of God's glory in the face of Jesus Christ" (II Corinthians 4:6b).

Isaiah dared to hope, dared to look ahead through the darkness of a nation's fallenness, dared to believe that some miracle child was coming out of who-knows-where to bring a new dawn, a new Kingdom unlike any other. And he was more on target than he could have ever known.

Isaiah not only announces the light; he describes the impact of it: endless peace, justice and righteousness. A few years ago, I saw an impact at the Carr P. Collins Center in Dallas. I saw a wide array of people who had come through the darkness. On the Sunday morning we gathered for worship, it did not take long for light to flood the place. The gospel choir was comprised primarily of the residents—alcoholics, drug addicts, the homeless, victims of unimaginable abuse, former convicts and prostitutes—people who had known the darkness in all its ugliness. And they sang. Oh, did they sing! I thought of Isaiah's words, "You have increased [their] joy" (v.3b)!

I recognized a lady I had seen sitting alone on my earlier tour. She had seemed before to be someone with no sense of self-worth. She had been a prostitute and had come to this place to find out if she could start over with God. When I saw her face in the choir, I saw someone released from an oppression. And I thought of Isaiah's words:

> You've shattered the yoke that burdened them, the staff
> on their shoulders, and the rod of their oppressor (v. 4).

"Mighty God," indeed!

There was another woman in the choir who had suffered years of domestic violence and had come to the center to find safety and peace. I saw her pull out a flute in the middle of a gospel song and play notes so smooth it felt like a healing balm being poured over our heads. The words of Isaiah were for her as well:

> Because every boot of the thundering warriors, and every garment rolled in blood will be burned, fuel for the fire. (v. 5)

I believe she was in the shelter of the Prince of Peace, the increase of whose government and peace there would, for her, be no end (v. 7).

The way Isaiah and all the prophets saw "government" was that it was based on a covenantal relationship, like a great big family where love is released by the everlasting Father, who establishes and upholds the Family "with justice and righteousness." And who is it for? That's the best part of all! Isaiah saw Zebulun and Naphtali, known in New Testament times as Galilee. Tribes humbled by heresy and compromise, scorned by Judah. A place where family members were long ago disowned.

That was where the light would most shine. That was where Jesus was to carry out most of His ministry. I saw the light in the faces of the gospel choir at Carr P. Collins. Yes, the light is for everyone, but it's only for everyone if it's for anyone in the darkest places of all, where the prisoners are set free, the humble are lifted up, and the hurting are healed.

Early on the morning of November 11, 1918, the citizens of Mons, Belgium, began to come out on the street. The machine guns were now silent; the German occupiers had retreated.

Someone yelled, "Hang out your flags!" The message was repeated throughout the city. When the sun rose, it shone brightly on a city of banners where the citizens had dwelt in darkness for four-and-a-half years and now walked free.

We, the people of God, are a city set free. The dawn has broken. The light has come. Let us hang out our flags and tell the world! Dance for joy! Hang out our flags and tell those oppressed by sin that the liberating Messiah has come! Tell a violent, abusing world that the Prince of Peace brings reconciliation! Hang out our flags for the Kingdom of God, where people love their enemies and live righteously. Hang out our flags, because we are the flag-bearers of a New World that started with a Child and will one day triumph completely—just as Isaiah said.

Prayer

Dear freedom-giving Lord, come again to our bondaged world. Speak Your liberating Word to our minds, release our hardened hearts from their captivity to our own interests, and shine Yourself through us to brighten this world with You, the Light of the World. I pray this through Jesus, for myself and for all Your people on this earth. Amen.

"A highway will be there. It will be called the Holy Way.... only the redeemed will walk in it" (Isaiah 35:8a, 9c).

WEEK TWO

TRUSTING GOD'S FUTURE

DECEMBER 4

Singing: Joy Will Return

Scripture—Isaiah 35:1-2a

The Israelites are exiled in Babylon. They are virtual slaves in a foreign land. Their joy has departed. What word is there to lift their spirits enough to see them through the ordeal? They find the words in the book of Isaiah. The prophecy is not launched with rational arguments to put minds at rest. It begins with singing. Isaiah sings about deserts and wilderness blossoming like the crocus, bursting into bloom, "rejoic[ing] with joy and singing." He sings the melodies of hope in a hopeless situation. I cannot imagine what it was like for those exiles to be waiting years for a deliverance for which they had no earthly guarantee nor observable signs. Could they believe Isaiah's optimism?

It isn't easy to sing when you are disheartened or despondent—unless, of course, you know a lament that matches your sadness. The Book of Isaiah and other prophetic books have plenty of laments that reflect God's sadness and anger over a nation's unfaithfulness and ungodly behavior. They are love songs laden with the grief of a rejected lover who longs for the loved one's return.

But this song is different. It flows in a major key. It dances to good news. It pulls us out of the doldrums. It drives away fear and claims victory even before the battle. Such songs are sung throughout the Old Testament, whether they are great anthems of praise at the dedication of the temple, or a terrifying songster brigade at the head of Jehoshaphat's victorious army, or Gideon's drum and bugle corps leveling the walls of Jericho, or the for-adults-only, extravagant love songs of Solomon. Some poets intimate that God sung all of creation into existence, launching a song that became a world and us, His beloveds. God speaks to us in song. When we turn from Him, He laments; when we follow His ways, He sings His pleasure.

He is the Pied Piper of a fallen world, luring us with His love song. Not some cheap, sentimental love song. No, a love song with pain and suffering and enormous sacrifice for us, His beloveds. And when we are lured by such a song, we answer:

> What language shall I borrow to thank Thee dearest Friend,
> for this Thy dying sorrow, Thy pity without end?
> O make me Thine forever! And should I fainting be,
> Lord, let me never, never, outlive my love to Thee.
>
> (Paulus Gerhardt, trans. James Waddell Alexander, *The Song Book of The Salvation Army*, 190, verse 3)

Such answering songs are sung from deep within us, from our souls. We are singing to our divine Lover; we are entrusting our lives to the One who gave His life for us. Even though our present circumstances may not seem to prove His loving presence, we believe that He will not abandon us, and that He has a future and a hope for us.

This is the kind of assurance the Israelites needed. God gave Isaiah the words and the music to sing His assurance of their future. It began with a vision of joy, sung with the imagery of new life bursting forth. It is a vision they could picture, because they had seen the world come to life in springtime. There was little joy under the ongoing circumstances, but there was joy in their future.

We live many centuries later. The Christ has now come in the flesh. But the world still "mourns in lowly exile." The joy we sing still directs us toward the future, to a promise still to be fulfilled. Yes, we feel the joy, but it doesn't settle us down as if the future has arrived. Rather, it pulls us forward and says that if we live the joy, it will spread far and wide, pulling others in.

Too often perhaps, we lose the joy, because we are depressed by a world being torn apart by hatred and violence, discouraged by the seeming complacency and dysfunction of other Christians, paralyzed by our own personal compromises and failures. There is plenty to rob us of our joy. And the lifelessness of some congregations can add to the sadness.

Almost three hundred years ago, when Isaac Watts was a teenager, he came home from a Sunday worship service complaining of how sad and solemn and dry the hymns sung by the congregation were. His father suggested he write some new hymns with more life and joy. He did—over six hundred of them over his lifetime! One of them is among the most buoyant of carols. Can you imagine not singing "Joy to the World" this season? We love to sing it in a loud voice and with a snappy tempo. We're singing with all of "Heaven and nature." The " … fields and floods, rocks, hills and plains/Repeat the sounding joy." It's a privilege we get to join in!

We should pay special attention to the second phrase in the carol: "The Lord is come." Not *has* come. *Is* come. The whole carol is in the present tense. It calls the "earth [to] receive her King" *now*. It calls us to open our hearts to Him today: "Let every heart prepare Him room." If we do not reopen our hearts to Him again this Advent season, how much meaning does the Bethlehem miracle two thousand years ago have for us? It would be a stale gift.

It seems to me this is the key to the last verse. The verse is a bold statement that Christ " ... rules the world with truth and grace,/ And makes the nations prove/The glories of His righteousness/And wonders of His love"—present tense. We do occasionally see glimpses of His rule and righteousness, but this world has a long, long way to go. Why is that? Perhaps the answer lies with Church inhabitants whose hearts do not prepare Him room. Christians locked within the dirge of a dull and compromised Christian religion. Christians who don't have the compassion and courage of a joyful heart. Christians who do not really sing while they march their witness into the world.

Isaiah saw the future, sang it, lived it—even though he didn't know when it would actually come. We do know the when. We do know that Christ was the fulfillment of the promise of a new Kingdom of love and righteousness. We are now called to sing Christ's new Kingdom with joy and live it with conviction. If enough of us do, that last verse of the carol will prove accurate. The glories of Christ's righteousness and the wonders of His love will become more and more apparent in a world moving toward Christ's Second Advent, when the kingdoms of this world will become the Kingdom of our Lord and of His Christ.

Prayer

God of hope, save me from a weakness of spirit that belittles my own ability to stand up against the bleakness around me and the influences of those forces that undermine Your Kingdom. Give me Your song and the courage to sing it in a strange land. Give me melodies that convey the joy that nothing can take away. Prepare my heart for a new and needed way for You to come to me this season. I pray this in the name of the Christ who drew me to Himself with a joyful love song I could no longer resist. Amen.

DECEMBER 5

Splendor: The Glory Will Break Through

Scripture—Isaiah 35:2bc

The prophecy of Isaiah now moves from joyous singing to the broader strokes of words like splendor and glory. "Splendor" suggests magnificence and grandeur, like the lush, fertile areas in Palestine of that day: Lebanon, Carmel and Sharon. "Glory" is a commonly used word in the Bible. The Hebrew originally had the sense of something heavy, and then developed further to mean wealth or abundance, esteem, dignity and honor. More and more, it came to be used to refer to God and was frequently used to express what humans saw when God revealed Himself to them. When Moses asked God to reveal His glory to him, he had to stand in the gap of a rock to keep from being shattered by it. Isaiah depicts a far more welcoming sight. We are invited to see it with wide-open eyes. There's nothing to hide from, everything to enjoy. It feels like escaping to the grandeur of the Rockies or the Appalachians, or the sand and sunny horizons of a Florida beach. Why is Isaiah comparing the glory of God to the natural beauty of Palestine's lush garden spots?

Isaiah, of course, was making a comparison—one that spoke to these captives who are living in a desert of isolation. They are far from home and the center of their Jewish faith. They are under the authority of a pagan ruler. They are lost. They are without a vision, and they are seeing no way forward. And Isaiah's prophecy has given them a vision of God's future by speaking of "the glory of Lebanon" and "the splendor of Carmel and Sharon" (v. 2b). They are not to think, however, that this is about a return to another Garden of Eden. The prophet is not speaking so much about a beautiful place as he is about the stunning beauty of God: "They will see the *Lord's* glory, the splendor of our *God*" (v. 2c., italics added).

We Christians use the word "glory" far more than "splendor." This probably has to do with the Latin word *gloria*, from which our English word is derived, and Latin was the language of Christian doctrine and music for most of the Western Church's history. The Old Testament rings with songs praising God's glory. Isaiah had a vision of the Lord high and lifted up, surrounded by winged creatures singing at the top of their lungs, and it sent him on a prophetic calling for the rest of his life (Isaiah 6:ff.). John the Divine had a similar vision and declared God "worthy . . . to receive glory and honor and power . . . " (Revelation 4:11).

The New Testament welcomes God's Son as the very reflection of God's glory: "God ... shone in our hearts to give us the light of the knowledge of God's glory in the face of Jesus Christ" (II Corinthians 4:6b). "To [Jesus Christ] belongs glory now and forever" (II Peter 3:18). His glory was revealed at His birth (Luke 2:9), by His miracles (John 2:11b), on the mount of transfiguration (Luke 9:32), on the cross (Galatians 6:14a) and at His resurrection (I Peter 1:21a). To Him is owed "glory and power forever and always" (Revelation 1:6b).

Does the Bible concede any glory to us who are created in the very image of God? As a matter of fact, it does. We are told that God made us " ... only slightly less than divine,/crowning [us] with glory and grandeur" (Psalm 8:5; Hebrews 2:7). We forfeited the glory, however, through our sin and irresponsibility. Christ came to our rescue by becoming one of us and tasting death for us. Now

He, not us, is the one crowned with glory (Hebrews 2:8-9).

How, then, do we find our dignity again? Like Paul, we take pride, not in our meager accomplishments but in our weaknesses (II Corinthians 11:30; 12:5). This makes no sense—until, like Paul, we give up our claims to self-sufficiency, in humility surrender to God's love and set out to glorify Him. Then we can hear Him make a promise He will always keep: "My grace is enough for you, because power is made perfect in weakness" (12:9).

So where do we go from there? First of all, we don't waste time bragging on ourselves; we brag on the Lord in His presence (Jeremiah 9:24; I Corinthians 1:29-31). We recognize that all human glory fades like the grass (Isaiah 40:6-7; I Peter 1:24), so we refuse to do good works for our own glory (Matthew 6:2). Whatever we do, we "do it all for God's glory" (I Corinthians 10:31). Our hope of glory is "Christ living in us" (Colossians 1:27b). The way we express our glory-giving to God is varied, but there is one way mentioned by Jesus that is intriguing. In His final prayer to the Father with His disciples before He is arrested, He says, "I've given them the glory that you gave me *so that they can be one just as we are one*" (John 17:22, italics added).

Perhaps the greatest tangible benefit of giving God glory is to unite the Body of Christ—the Church, our corps (a Salvation Army church congregation, from Latin *corpus*, a body, as in "the Body of Christ"). Perhaps your own corps is divided by competitive glory-seeking. Perhaps some members waste time comparing themselves to one another. Perhaps there are cliques that shut out others, gossip incessantly or refuse to reach out to "less attractive" members, other attendees or occasional visitors. Perhaps you realize you haven't had the courage to name this divisiveness, or you humbly realize you have occasionally participated in it. What Jesus' prayer teaches us is that our divisiveness demeans God Himself by making our claims to glorify Him a sham. It is empty praise, an insult to the Christ who confessed the longing of His heart when He prayed of us: "I pray they will be one, Father, just as You are in me and I am in You" (v. 21a). He goes on to pray that this unity of the Father with the Son will also make possible the credibility of our witness in the world (v. 21b).

So much hangs on our praise and the humility it must entail if it is genuine. As Isaiah called upon a people to humble themselves in praise as well as to allow praise to humble them, so Christ calls us, His disciples today, to humble ourselves so the glory will break through. This could be the beginning of new health for our corps and the credibility for our mission. This Advent, why not wait eagerly for such a miracle? In fact, why not start living as if it was already happening?

Prayer

God of glory, I praise You for Your undeserved goodness and grace in my life. I thank You for sending Christ to teach me how to love and praise You. I confess that my love has sometimes been superficial and my praise sometimes perfunctory. Help me to love You in a way that sings with praise, and to praise You in a way that fills me to overflowing with Your love. May this Advent season teach me to sing my praises like the angels at Jesus' birth and come to You in awe and wonder like humble hillside shepherds. I pray this in the name of the Christ who came at Bethlehem and will keep coming in new ways, until He comes in glory. Amen.

DECEMBER 6

Strength: Power Will Be Restored

Scripture—Isaiah 35:3-4a

Isaiah's words speak power to a people who feel powerless. The captive Israelites have not only been overpowered by a stronger nation; they have been brought back by their captors to Babylon to serve the interests of their conquerors. They have been forcibly taken from their homeland. These two verses tell them to do some stunning things: transcend their powerlessness, strengthen their grip on their lives, and firm the steadiness of their stance. There is a power no one can take from them. If they live in that power, they will be strong and fear will not weaken them. Their social status will still be marked as captive and slave, but the status of their hearts will be free and unbroken.

Nelson Mandela served decades in an inhuman island prison, because he relentlessly fought for full citizenship for native South Africans. John McCain survived years of cruel torture as a prisoner of war in a North Vietnamese concentration camp. Dietrich Bonhoeffer risked his life to remove Hitler from power, was caught and imprisoned, and eventually hanged. All three of these heroes proved in the end to be more powerful than the political strength of oppressive governments. Where did that strength come from? How did they deal with their fear?

There is a strength that comes from secure surroundings, economic prosperity, political power and protection from enemies. These men had none of these props in their captivity. There is another strength that comes from within, a strength that endures and even prospers when the sources of the other strength are removed. It is a strength from deep within a person's soul that enables him or her to take huge risks for a higher good or for the lives of other people. It doesn't panic; it doesn't give in to fear; it doesn't feel powerless (v. 4a).

You know what fear is, and so do I. I've known for a long time. I knew fear when our eldest daughter turned sixteen, and I handed her the car keys for her first drive alone, and it was night. I knew fear when our car hit an oil slick on a curve after a rain and spun out of control. I knew fear when I became a Salvation Army officer and wondered if I could really do what was required. I still know fear. I sometimes fear failure and embarrassment, and at my age, I fear the possibility that I could become helpless and handicapped for years before I die.

If we're honest with ourselves, we will admit that there are certain things that all of us do fear. Fear is a natural emotion. It is an instinct God gives us to be aware of dangerous or threatening situations so that we can either avoid them or be prepared to confront them. Fear is God's gift for our safety. We may wonder, then, why Isaiah was telling the Israelites *not* to fear, rather than warning them of the threats they faced and advising them how to avoid them. Certainly they had plenty to be afraid of!

Isaiah must have been on to something else—likely a word from the Lord. I have learned from reading the Bible that when God or His spokesperson—a prophet, an apostle or an angel—tells the one or ones being addressed, "Don't fear," it means He is going to do something important on their behalf. It may come to pass soon, or it may take years. If they are persecuted for their faith, their fear, though real, is superseded by their awareness that their God will be with them whether the outcome is life or death. Their hands may be weak, but they will be strengthened. Their knees may be unsteady, but they will be supported. No need to panic. God will strengthen them.

What is this God-given strength, and where does it come from? It comes from what God does in our hearts. It flows from the heart of Jesus on the cross. It is the strength of love—the strength that no earthly power can overcome. It enabled the Israelites to love their God by loving their families, their faith community and even their enemies. In the end, the power of God's love won. In the end, the love of power lost.

If the love of power is what drives me, I will see love as a transferable commitment based on what attracts me most that day. My transactions with people will take place primarily on the basis of outcomes that serve me best. My votes will be cast for candidates and policies that will best advance my own security and prosperity. This is how the love of power works. It is power for me, my family, my race or ethnicity, or my nation.

This is not the power Isaiah says God wants to restore. Because it pursues only one's self-interest, it is based on fear of other people, fear of enemies, fear of the unknown and fear of the future. The Jews had been called by God to be a blessing to the other nations—not to be a closed, frightened society interested only in its own survival and certainly not to be a world dominating power. The power being restored was the courage and strength to carry out that calling in the future—and for the time being as well. It was a calling to trust the power of their powerlessness.

Jesus' calling was the same, with one major and decisive revelation: *the power of powerlessness is the power of love.* Jesus is the embodiment of God's love for the world (John 3:16), the self-giving love that saves (v.17). It is the self-giving love that refuses to allow fear to have the upper hand. It has no fear; in fact, it casts out fear (I John 4:18). Isaiah's command to "Be strong! Don't fear!" is an invitation to listen to the self-giving love song of the God who will not abandon us. In Jesus, it became the love song of the life He gave us, the strength He withheld to save us, the power to love He bequeathed to us. Yes, power will be restored—the power to love as Jesus did, so that the world may be saved.

Prayer

Powerful and loving Father, we thank You for the life and example of Jesus, who used His power for others and not Himself, and who became powerless so as to release such an overflow of love as to provide for the world's desperate spiritual thirst. Save me from the temptation to seize power for my own security and self-advancement. Teach me to surrender such power, so that Your love can live in me and in others. I pray this in the name of the one who gave up earthly power to release the power of redeeming love—our Savior, Jesus the living Christ. Amen.

DECEMBER 7

SALVATION: GOD WILL COME TO THE RESCUE

Scripture—Isaiah 35:4bc

Something big is afoot! NIV renders it in a confident future tense: "Your God will come." CEB in the affirmative present: "Here's your God." One is assurance that God will indeed act; the other is the claim that He is already present and at work. Both are true: God is already involved in the world on our behalf, and He will continue to act in the days and years to come. What exactly He is up to is found at the end of the verse: "God will come to save you."

For the Jewish exiles in Babylon, that 'saving' had specific meaning. It is described with many images in the verses that follow, but here it is summed up in the word 'rescue.' The exiles wanted to be freed from their captors and return home. Rescue, however, would not come quickly. What could they do in the meantime? They could trust in their rescue, even if delayed for years, and they could start living in their captivity as if they were free. What does that mean?

Jeremiah's letter to the exiles in Babylon gives us good clues (Jeremiah 29:4-15). He tells them to settle down, build houses, cultivate their gardens for food, get married, have babies. In other words, increase their numbers and influence. Become a part of the life of their captors, be good citizens. Position themselves so that their faith in God will rub off on people. In fact, seek the *shalom* (peace, prosperity) of the city. Pray for it. The plans I have in mind for you, says the Lord, are "plans for peace, not disaster, to give you a future filled with hope. When . . . you pray to Me, I will listen to you. When you search for Me, yes, search for Me with all your heart, you will find Me. I will be present for you . . . and I will bring you home after your long exile . . ."

Advent is not just about waiting. It is about waiting as if God is already at work, preparing new ways for us to get on board by becoming witnesses and influencers for the Kingdom of God. We wait for God by living and acting for God. One of the most damaging failures of the Christian Church over its long history is its passivity: leaving everything up to God while we have worship, enjoy our fellowship with one another, pray for one another, perhaps let a few new people in to our congregation each year to try to compensate for those who leave or die. We do not live in hope this way. We live without hope. God's aim is the salvation of the world. He is not satisfied with our cozy few. To be truthful, He is probably disgusted.

The apostle Paul knew that in Jesus the Christ, deliverance had arrived. It was as if Jesus had entered the Babylons of our captivity, releasing us from the powers that held us and preparing us for our eventual return to our true home. Paul knew that the challenge and privilege of the follower of this rescuing Jesus was now living out this new freedom in an oppressive and unholy world. He gives plenty of guidance on the matter. In the letter to the Roman Church he speaks of their not being "conformed to the patterns of this world" and in genuine humility using their respective gifts to strengthen one another. He doesn't stop there. He goes on to encourage Christians to welcome strangers into their homes, bless those who harass them for their faith, consider all people as equals, associate with the marginalized, refrain from repaying evil with evil, as best as one can live at peace with all people, resist the urge to seek revenge, love their enemies, and defeat evil with good. (see Romans 12) Tall order, indeed!

We are rescued to become part of the rescue effort. So what does the rescue plan look like? Paul seems to arrive at the heart of the matter in the thirteenth chapter. First comes the non-negotiable principle: "Don't be in debt to anyone, except for the obligation to love each other" (Rom. 13:8a). Then comes the startling revelation that in doing so, we are actually *fulfilling* the Law (vv. 8b, 10b). In other words, what the Law really intends is not to make us legalists, measuring ourselves and others by compliance with the trivial details. The Law's real intention is to help us become lovers of God and of others. We live in this gospel rescue, this salvation God has given us by His grace in Jesus, by becoming what Brengle called "love slaves"—participants in what God is doing to rescue this world from its oppression and people from their enslavement. We the rescued become hands of our Lord in His rescue enterprise.

In the year 1951, J.D. Salinger wrote a novel about Holden Caulfield entitled *The Catcher in the Rye*. Holden is the teenage son of a well-to-do New York City couple, and he has just succeeded in getting kicked out of yet another private school. He's not a terrible misfit. He's a lost soul who can't seem to take anything seriously, can't find his place in the world, and can't find anything worth devoting his life to. He's a kid who at times sounds suicidal.

There's a point in the story when he's talking to his little sister, Phoebe—one of the very few people in his life he loves and respects. Exasperated and pained by her irresponsible brother, Phoebe shouts out at him, "Name something you'd like to be." Just name *something*. Holden's answer was probably quoted by half the preachers in this country during the 60s and 70s. It's worth quoting again:

> You know that song "If a body catch a body comin' through the rye," [said Holden]... I keep picturing all these little kids playing some game in this big field of rye and all. Thousands of little kids, and nobody's around—nobody big,

I mean—except me. And I'm standing on the edge of some crazy cliff. What I have to do, I have to catch everybody if they start to go over the cliff—I mean if they're running and don't look where they're going, I have to come out from somewhere and *catch* them. That's all I'd do all day. I'd just be the catcher in the rye and all. I know it's crazy, but that's the only thing I'd really like to be. I know it's crazy.

When he has failed to find meaning in just about everything else, this young but broken soul finds something that takes hold of his heart. Sadly, the story doesn't tell us if Holden ever finds a way to live out this passion to be a rescuer of the vulnerable. We who are followers of Jesus, however, are all qualified and recruited for His rescue mission. Through His enabling grace, we the rescued become Christ's rescuers. It's also what being a Salvationist means.

Prayer
God of our salvation, thank You for sending Jesus to rescue us from the emptiness of a loveless existence. Thank You for calling me to be part of Your mission to save the world. Keep alive in me the memory of my former enslavements and the miracle of Your saving work in my life. Save me from a falsely holy absorption in myself and my so-called accomplishments. Free me to live well in, and not of, a world captivated by sin. Enable me to do so with the compassion of Christ and the discernment of the Holy Spirit. Make me a rescuer in the field of Your mission, I pray in the name of our beloved Rescuer. Amen.

DECEMBER 8

RESTORATION: HEALING WATERS WILL FLOW

Scripture—Isaiah 35:5-6ab

Quite abruptly, Isaiah's prophecy moves from rescue to healing: the blind now able to see, the deaf to hear, the lame to leap like the deer, the dumb to speak. God's future is a place of disabilities removed. Well, when will that future come? When will healing waters flow?

Is this false hope, a cruel promise? Or does it speak to healing for all of us? We all need healing, don't we? Did not the prophet say that the sun of righteousness would "rise with healing in its wings" (Malachi 4:2, NIV)? Did not Jesus "heal . . . every disease and sickness among the people" (Matthew 4:23)? The Gospels paint a vivid picture of restored health. Our brokenness, our lack of wholeness, may not be those specifically mentioned by Isaiah. They are nonetheless real. We all need restoration. During this Advent season, we prepare ourselves for Christ's coming anew into our lives and into our world. Should this not also include a new healing?

There is real division among Christians over the relationship between spiritual healing and both emotional and physical healing. At one extreme are those Christians who claim that the failure of a follower of Jesus to receive either emotional or physical healing prayed for is probably due to inadequate faith on the person's part. At the other extreme are Christians who see no connection whatever between one's spiritual health and one's emotional or physical health. One group sees healing as faith-based magic; the other sees healing, when it happens, as scientifically explainable. And in between these extremes are other views, usually leaning more in one direction than the other.

I think it's helpful to approach the matter of God's healing by exploring the relationship between holiness and wholeness. A verse in our *Song Book* (387, anon) has these two lines:

Bad as I was He cleansed my soul,
Healed my disease and made me whole.

These lines connect holiness ("cleansed my soul"), healing ("healed my disease") and wholeness ("made me whole"). The Tenth Article of our Doctrines is based on the prayer of I Thessalonians 5:23, which petitions for "the God of peace [to] sanctify us wholly [or through and through]." The term used in our Tenth Article is "wholly sanctified." That phrase is usually interpreted either as perfectly sanctified (all faults gone) or as on-the-way-to-perfection sanctified—or as a combination of the two. The latter part of the verse prays for our "spirit, soul, and body" to be kept intact or under guard and blameless at our Lord Jesus Christ's coming.

That last part is interesting. When we are sanctified, all parts of our lives are touched and transformed. God the Sanctifier and God the Healer are one and the same God, and holiness and wholeness are one indivisible benefit of His saving work. This obviously does not mean that the truly sanctified will automatically be relieved of all bodily ailments and disabilities, although healings do sometimes take place. Nor does it mean that emotional damage incurred earlier in life is necessarily completely done away with, although the Holy Spirit and caring friends and counselors can help the person find and live out of his truer self in Christ.

December 8

The sanctifying grace of God allows us to live with our emotional baggage and physical disabilities, while not giving them the last word in defining who we are or determining how we act. We all have our wounds and limitations, and when a body of believers—for example, a corps—accepts this reality, members can be healing influences on each other, and I think God would consider such a corps a very healthy and whole Body of Christ.

Some people are in particular need of *spiritual* healing. They haven't really allowed God to forgive them. They don't know that beholding the glory of God in the face of Christ, they can be transformed into His image (II Cor. 3:18). They need to know that without doubt, God heals the broken spirit and sanctifies the erring heart. They need to claim the gift of soul cleansing.

Others are in need of *relational* healing. Almost immediately following the Genesis account of the Fall, the Scriptures commence an extended parade of broken relationships. We break our relationship with God, and our relationships with one another are also broken. What Scripture makes clear is that the health of our relationships with God cannot be separated from our relationships with others. John the Apostle puts it in stark words: "If anyone says, I love God, and hates a brother or sister, he is a liar, because the person who doesn't love a brother or sister who can be seen can't love God, who can't be seen" (I John 4:20). Some Christians are stuck in relational problems. They may know that God heals the broken spirit, but they are unable to claim the healing of their broken relationships. They can't bring themselves fully to trust another, to pay the price of risking hurt, to trust the power of a caring relationship without the need to mask or manipulate.

There are others who need *emotional* healing. Their emotions are damaged in some way, their hearts broken. Depression haunts them, and suppressed emotions sap their strength. They are true sufferers and need healing as much as anyone.

And there are those who need *physical* healing. We have two great needs in this area. The first is to believe that God can and wants to heal us. Whatever form that healing takes may not meet all of our expectations. In fact, we differ significantly in our levels of physical health and ability. A person with limiting disability or disease, however, may well be a healthier person than someone in perfect physical shape, seen through the eyes of God. The second need is to accept responsibility for our own health. It's neither fair nor sensible for us to ask God to heal our bodies when we ourselves refuse to treat them as a part of His creation by taking care of them.

We are participants in our own healing, whether the healing is spiritual, emotional, relational or physical. Perhaps this Advent, you will want to seek and prepare for healing from the Christ who will visit us again.

Prayer

Dear Lord, this Advent I seek the restorative power of Jesus in my own life. I ask the Christ who healed the sick and the disabled to bring healing where I so much need and desire it: (Name the healing you seek_____). I trust You, Lord, to heal me in the way You know best, and I commit myself to do my part in receiving the healing, living my life by it and giving witness to it. I pray this in the name of Jesus, my Healer and Lord. Amen.

DECEMBER 9

Refreshment: Thirst Will Be Quenched

Scripture—Isaiah 35:6c-7

In the previous meditation, we looked at Isaiah's prophecy of a time of cleansing and healing. He now turns to our thirst, and his words describe a cascade of life-giving refreshment:

> Waters will spring up in the desert, and streams in the wilderness.
> The burning sand will become a pool, and the thirsty ground, fountains of water.
> The jackal's habitat, a pasture; grass will become reeds and rushes.

What he is describing is a miracle: water flowing from the least place you'd expect—a desert of dry, burning sand. In much of Palestine, water readily accessible *was* a miracle. And when periods of drought came, life was in danger.

Earlier in the book, Isaiah used the imagery of a drought to depict the deadly outcome of Israel's sin. He saw Zion as "a withering oak, like a garden without water," catching fire and burning (1:30-31). "The waters of the sea will dry up;/the rivers will be parched and bare" (19:5). Even when there was water in the cistern, the Lord could break the storage jar that drew it and deny access (30:14b). As if the threat of death by lack of water wasn't enough, the prophet reversed the equation and spoke of the danger of drowning in the flood from a sudden rainstorm (28:2). The waters can, indeed, be our oppressors (30:20). We can die from lack of water, and we can die from its overwhelming, perhaps from the hoarding of our resources (Luke 12:15-21).

Water is a symbol of refreshment. It revives and refreshes us. When the children of Israel were severely dehydrated during their forty-year wilderness journey, Jehovah told Moses to strike the rock, and water gushed out (48:21). The poor have no water, but the Lord will respond and not abandon them (41:17). True servants of the Lord will be refreshed, but idolaters will thirst (65:13c). The promise is given to Israel in 44:3:

> I will pour out water on thirsty ground and streams upon dry land.
> I will pour out my spirit upon your descendants and my blessing upon your offspring.

Indeed, the Lord Himself will be "like a watered garden,/like a spring that won't run dry" (58:11). And the invitation echoes around the world to the whosoever: "All of you who are thirsty, come to the waters" (55:1). Come home to God.

We all know what it means to be thirsty. I remember the time when I was the thirstiest I think I've ever been. I was about nine years old, and it was summer. It was the best summer of my childhood. My Salvation Army officer parents were on the Training College staff and, as was the case with all staff officers at the time, they were given other assignments during the summer break. Their assignment was to run the Territorial Camp Grandview. It was heaven on earth for me—endless adventures in a mountainous area of North Georgia with minimal supervision! There were a number of "firsts" for me that summer. Among them was learning how to fish and finding a measure of success with it; I became so intrigued with aquatic life that my original intent in going to university was to major in marine biology. Also, for the first time, I saw a chicken running around with its head cut off. It freaked me out! I also noticed campers who were sweet on each other walking around holding hands, and I figured there must be something to such behavior, and someday I might be able to find out.

Perhaps my most heroic effort that summer was to climb Sharp Top Mountain for the first time. The camp lay a relatively short walk from the base of the mountain, and though the Camp had not been owned by the Army for long, climbing Sharp Top had already become the thing for campers and supervising adults to do to prove something—virility, strength, manhood, or something like that. Between camps, a couple of the adult staff, my brother Walter and I decided to make the climb. We, of course, were going to go up on the steep side—the greater challenge. Unfortunately, on the way down, we walked over an unseen yellow jacket nest and were immediately attacked. We started running helter-skelter down that mountain as fast as we could. We had taken no water with us, and I had forgotten to drink plenty of water before we left for the hike. By the time we reached the base of the mountain, my mouth was parched. I was desperate for water. As it happened, we came across a pipe gushing with water protruding from an outcropping of rocks. I put my mouth in the way of it and swallowed for a blessed eternity. Seventy years later, I can still taste the purity, still feel the overwhelming refreshment. Water poured on the thirsty ground of my tired, parched body.

The very word refreshment says that we need a fresh supply, or we will become depleted. If we don't refresh ourselves, we will die. This is not only true for our physical prosperity; it is also true for our spiritual health, where life-giving refreshment comes from the

Christ who has "the living water" to give us (John 4:10)—a spring that "bubbles up into eternal life" (4:14b). A Christian who doesn't continue to partake of Christ is a Christian who will dehydrate like "a withering oak." And what does our refreshing Christ tell us to do with our lives? First, He tells us to find and give refreshment to our brothers and sisters in Christ. The apostle Paul looks forward to seeing Philemon so as to "refresh my heart in Christ" (Philemon 20b). He refreshes the Philippians with his letter of gratitude and instruction, while at the same time drawing strength and spiritual sustenance from them.

Our Lord gives us water not only to refresh ourselves; He gives it also to share generously with others. Fools deprive the thirsty of drink, says Isaiah (32:6d). Jesus assures us that "…everybody who gives even a cup of cold water to these little ones because they are My disciples will certainly be rewarded" (Matthew 10:42). We are called to give a refreshing drink to the thirsting Jesus we see in "the least of these" (25:35b). It is a sobering thought that those who hoard their resources of refreshment from those whose bodies or souls are dry, are unworthy of eternity. This Advent season, as you prepare yourself for the coming of Christ, you may want to partake more deeply of His water of life for your soul, and you may also want to discover and pursue new ways to share that refreshment with the thirsty people all around you.

Prayer

Dear Lord, Giver and Sustainer of life, refresh me with Your Spirit this Advent season. Prepare me to receive the gift of Your living water, sharpen my vision to see the thirst of those around me, and expand my compassion to share refreshment from my storehouse and from my heart. Through Jesus Christ my Lord, source of the water of life. Amen.

DECEMBER 10

A Highway: The Way Will Be Found

Scripture—Isaiah 35:8-10

Over the previous seven verses, Isaiah has been describing in vivid imagery what lay in the exiles' future after the years of the embarrassment and the suffering resulting from their banishment to Babylon. He spoke of joy, singing, glory, splendor, strength and salvation. He painted a picture of a blossoming desert, the blind seeing, the deaf hearing, the dumb talking, the lame jumping like deer, streams in the wilderness and pools of refreshing water in the desert. These will be God's gifts to them. There will, however, be one more gift, different from the others. The prophet describes it in verses 8-10. It is the gift of a road to travel on the way to their promised future:

A highway will be there.
It will be called The Holy Way. (v.8a)

Evidently, this is not a highway for anyone who wants an easy, comfortable way to travel. It is a highway only for the ransomed and redeemed (vv. 10a, 9d). The unclean will not travel on it (v. 8b). Predators will not be able to enter it (v. 9a). The travelers will return to Zion and enter it "...with singing, with everlasting joy upon their heads./Happiness and joy will overwhelm them; grief and groaning will flee away" (v.10). This is not a busy interstate for just anyone. It is the narrow way for those who are ready to emerge from their self-centered—and therefore destructive—lives. They qualify to travel, not by their own merit, not even any merit of their suffering, but by the ransom paid and the redemption given by God Himself. Their return is not to their old, faithless way of life; they do not pick up where they left off. They now travel a very different way called "The Holy Way."

We who are followers of Jesus must not miss the profound significance of this metaphor of our lives as a journey. The Christian life is not a settled existence. It is a way to travel. We do not "maintain" our Christian faith. We grow in it. Christians who have been in the same place spiritually for years are actually not in the same place. They are in a worse place, just as any living thing that hasn't grown in the growing season has inevitably deteriorated. Albert Orsborn said it well in Song 430 of our *Song Book*: For the Christian, "Life is a journey; [and] long is the road." It is "a seeking... a quest... [and] a finding." In the chorus of the song, Orsborn acknowledges that this spiritual journey is made possible only by our allowing ourselves to be nurtured by the Spirit and refreshed by Christ, "the water of life." The journey is not a blind, impulsive rush to cover as much ground as is humanly possible; it is a pilgrimage with Christ and fellow disciples who encourage, support and nurture us. Bystanders can hear us singing the joyful songs of Zion. Furthermore, as we travel this new way of life, we invite those very bystanders to become fellow travelers with Christ.

The freed captives of Babylon were not being given a free pass to wherever they chose to go. They were presented with the route called holiness. It was not to be a walk in the park. There were still dangers, but they were not to be feared. "Don't be afraid, little flock," says Jesus to us, "because your Father delights in giving you the Kingdom" (Luke 12:32). Our journey is the way of holiness. Jesus called it living in the Kingdom of God, our true home and way of life. And He gave Himself, soul and body, to open the way to us (Hebrews 10:20).

This Advent season, we once again await the coming of Christ. We await His appearing today. Today, He will come as He did before—in an unlikely place, perhaps at an inconvenient time, to unlikely recipients like you and me. He will likely reveal something new about how we will continue our journey on the way of holiness. For some, He will extend the invitation to join the journey for the first time. For others, He will plead that they return to the journey from which they have strayed. For all of us, His companionship is assured, His presence almost tangible. Today, He is with us every step of the way (Matthew 28:20b).

We also await Christ's final coming in glory. Our whole lives move toward that future. We do not, however, simply wait. Far from it. We live it *now*. We take the Holy Way today. That is what makes our motivations, attitudes, lifestyle and actions so foreign in a world wired very differently. We look around for evidence of God's Kingdom, and when we find it, we rejoice and support it. Unfortunately, most of what we see is not the Kingdom of God. So we refuse to go along with it, or we confront it, and we hope our lives will delegitimize it. Strange as our way of life seems in the world in which we live most of our days, we are demonstrating "the new normal" inaugurated by Jesus' life and redemptive death. And if we live well this new life of engaged holiness, we will be sending messages to the hearts of those we touch. Some will indeed realize that this Lord and this life are what they so deeply long for, and they may well take the risk of joining the journey with Christ. This, in fact, is our mission.

Many years ago, Thomas Carlyle, the Scottish essayist, and his friend Bishop Wilberforce of the Church of England were discussing the subject of death. Somewhere in the discussion, Carlyle asked his friend, "Bishop, do you have a creed?" Wilberforce replied at once: "Yes, I do have a creed, and the older I grow, the firmer it becomes; but there's one thing that staggers me about my creed." "What's that?" asked Carlyle. The Bishop answered, "It's the slow progress that my creed makes in the world." Carlyle remained silent for a few moments, and then, slowly and seriously, he said, "Ah, but if you have a creed, you can afford to wait."

Many Christians long for Christ's return to come soon. Some are so world-weary and impatient that they buy into the predictions of self-proclaimed prophets who say the time is very, very near. A few even venture to give a date. They miss the point, which is that *Christ calls us to live every day as if He were coming that very day.* Then there is no need to speculate, only to live the life of Jesus in the world—which is to say, to journey on the Holy Way and be imitators of Christ with sufficient likeness to make a real difference in the world. The goal is not primarily the triumph of our creed, as Wilberforce suggested; it is Christ's continuing transformation of our lives (Romans 12:2) and of the world (Revelation 21:1). Our calling is the privilege to participate and facilitate.

Prayer

Living Lord, I long for the day when Your Kingdom will come in its fullness. Save Your people from the distraction of speculation about Your coming. Help me to live every day of my life as if You were coming that very day, as sure as the morning glow on the eastern horizon signals a new sunrise. I ask You to wash away any impurity in my life, fill me with the love that casts out any fears that sap my courage, and empower me humbly to travel the way called holiness. I pray this in the name of Jesus, my Liberator and Guide on the journey of my life. Amen

"So let's get rid of the actions that belong to the darkness and put on the weapons of light" (Romans 13:12b).

WEEK THREE
PREPARING FOR CHANGE

DECEMBER 11

SELF-DOUBTING: THE BARRIER TO CHANGE

Scripture—Luke 1:5-24a; 59-80

Zechariah had everything going for him. He was a priest in the highly respectable line of Abijah. His wife, Elizabeth, was a descendant of the priestly line of Aaron—yes, *the* Aaron, whose wife was also named Elizabeth. He had, as we say, the bloodline, the training and the credentials. That's not all he had going for him. He and Elizabeth were " ... both righteous before God, blameless in their observance of all the Lord's commandments and regulations." In terms of their religious practices, they seem entitled and qualified for whatever special calling the Lord might have for them. As it turns out, the Lord did have an incredibly important calling, and He was about to lay it on Zechariah, with the help of an angel named Gabriel. He and Elizabeth were to conceive and bear a son who would be a joy and a delight to them, as well as to many people. Gabriel said that son would be filled with the Holy Spirit and live a disciplined, God-fearing life. He would bring many Israelites back to God and begin a revival of righteousness the likes of which the world had never seen. He would do this to make ready a people prepared for the Lord. He was to be a second Elijah announcing the long-awaited Messiah! "And by the way, Zechariah," said Gabriel, "you will not give him your name, as people would expect. You will name him John."

Zechariah was startled—obviously overcome by this message. His mind, however, kept going back to Gabriel's *opening* line—the part about Elizabeth conceiving a child. It would take a miracle for elderly Elizabeth to conceive, and Zechariah was probably unsure of his ability to do *his* part in the process. On the face of it, it seemed—and was likely to be—a setup for failure. "Give me some assurance, show me a sign, Gabriel! Some convincing proof we very senior citizens, who have never been able to conceive all these years, are now equal to the task." "You want a sign, Zechariah?" asks the Lord's messenger. "Here it is: '. . . you will remain silent, unable to speak until the day when these things happen.'" When Zechariah emerged from the temple, he had no speech—only gestures—and he could not give the waiting faithful the traditional blessing. They concluded the truth: he must have seen a stunning vision.

It is a daring act of faith to believe in miracles—even more so when you are told you will be the instrument of a miracle you never imagined and could not see as possible, given the proven lack of success of miracles. True, Zechariah was ardently hoping and praying for the advent of the long-prophesied Messiah. He was certainly aware that a prophet like Elijah would forerun and announce this Messiah. But the idea that he and Elizabeth could possibly conceive a son at that time was a huge stretch, even for this pious priest.

The nature of miracles is that there is no rational or scientific explanation for them. God sometimes, and more often than we think, invades our lives and bypasses the explainable with unmistakable excesses of His love—as was the promised miracle now revealed to Zechariah. God was about to fulfill a longstanding promise—a promise Zechariah deeply believed would come to pass someday. He even hoped it would come in his lifetime. His problem was that he knew too much. He knew the elderly can't bear children and certainly not after decades of trying. Rational minds agreed with him. So he asked for a sign, and he got a muting—the silencing of his doubt. His silence spoke. Something holy happened, and the people saw it in his face.

Luke's description of what followed is surprisingly straightforward and unadorned. Zechariah completed the days of this priestly assignment in the temple and went home—and Elizabeth became pregnant. We are being drawn to see the *real story*. It was not about Zechariah's ability to father a child. It was not about Elizabeth's womb. It was about God's faithfulness to His people and to His world. It was about the prepared-for Son that was about to come into the world and become the embodied mission of God to save us. And it began with this voice crying in the wilderness named John, born improbably as a miracle child of fierce nerve and passion, whom God used to get our attention and turn us to Jesus.

Jesus is the miracle. God-with-us-in-the-flesh is the miracle. The Incarnation is the miracle. And it will play itself out all the way to a saving cross and a stunning resurrection.

Nine months later, John was born and given a non-family name that said he would not be following in his father's occupational footsteps. He would not serve in the temple; he would serve on the rough roads of wilderness—the places where common people and sinners gathered, confessed their sins and were baptized—all of it in preparation for the true Messiah, Jesus. Jesus would open the door to God's real agenda: for us to be saved through, become lovers of, and live in the holiness of Jesus Himself. By the time John was born, Zechariah saw clearly that John would be a prophet of the Most High who would go before this saving Lord and prepare His way. (Check out his bold prophecies in verses 67-79!)

The self-doubter became the believer. Zechariah teaches us that the good news about our self-doubts is that we can get beyond them. To be sure, our doubting is often a good use of our minds to keep us from getting sucked in by false pretenses and con jobs. It is sometimes an honest response to the questionable or the unlikely. Our self-doubts are different. They are not expressions of a humble spirit; they are a cowardice of the soul, a fear of being made the fool, a self-imprisonment in past failures. The Bible is full of self-doubters like Moses, Gideon, Jeremiah, and now, Zechariah. They began without courage and then allowed their fears of failure to be replaced by risks of faith in God and what He was about to do through them—woefully inadequate vessels though they were.

The doubts that defeat us are not so much of the mind as of the heart. One poet called our doubts traitors that cause us to lose the good we might have gained by fearing to attempt. We are all Zechariahs—painfully aware of our inadequacies and failings. And God is waiting for us to trust Him to do the seemingly impossible—and help Him change the world.

Prayer

Dear Lord and Master of the impossible, give me the confidence to trust You above my own self-doubting. Give me the fortitude not to dismiss outright the opportunity to dare to accept an exceptional challenge for Your Kingdom. Grant me the courage to accept Your call to advance the mission of Jesus, even if there is the possibility of embarrassment or even failure. I ask this through Jesus and trusting in His adequacy. Amen.

DECEMBER 12

BELIEVING: THE DOOR TO CHANGE

Scripture—Luke 1:24-25; 39-45, 56-60

We are not told what communication, if any, transpired between Zechariah and Elizabeth when he returned from his temple duty. A priest without his speech is seriously handicapped in performing his priestly duties. A husband unable to talk to his wife is reduced to everyday gestures and exaggerated lip movements. As with the crowd outside the temple, Elizabeth surely sensed something extraordinary had happened—so extraordinary it muted her beloved with the power of it. Perhaps he used the meager means of communication he had available to convey as best he could what he saw and heard. Or perhaps the look in his eyes, or the silence that marked him, or the mystery that seemed to possess him, said all that needed to be said. Visions are hard to explain, especially when they ask of the visionary what seems to be undoable on his or her part. But they are life-changing, and I suspect that Elizabeth knew it.

Elizabeth—I wish we knew more about her. These verses are the only mention of her in the New Testament. We know that as a woman of that day and culture, her primary social value was to have and raise children. Childlessness brought shame on a married woman, as if infertility was a condition of women alone, which we now know isn't the case. Luke doesn't describe Elizabeth's embarrassment over her childlessness; he doesn't need to. All he has to say is "Elizabeth was unable to have children."

What we know about Elizabeth is that her name in Hebrew means "to whom God is the oath." To *Elizabeth*, God is the oath. The word "oath" has two meanings. One is an appeal to God or some other "higher power" to confirm that a statement is true. The other is the use of God's name as a swearword or a curse. A childless woman might well swear an oath in the second sense to vent her anger at God over her inability to conceive or bring the child she carried in her womb to term. The first meaning could describe the deep belief of a married woman that God would grant her what she was expected to be able to do—namely, to bear children.

Elizabeth's name suggests yet a different understanding of the oath. God *was* her oath. She did not so much appeal to God for this or that desirable thing, as she simply and implicitly trusted Him. If God did not intervene to give her children, she trusted Him still. Her oath was not a statement of provable truth; it was her deep trust in a Person, no matter what. When she learned that she was pregnant, she didn't shout out: "I *knew* it! I knew God would give me this child I so much wanted!" What she said was a recognition that her pregnancy was not His relenting to her endless pleading. It is what the God she trusted had intended for her all along. It was His grace and favor. "This," she said, "is the Lord's doing."

In the sixth month of Elizabeth's pregnancy, the angel Gabriel appeared again—this time to Elizabeth's teenage cousin Mary in Nazareth. The message given to her was similar; she also would become pregnant, even though she was only engaged to an older man named Joseph. But that wouldn't be a problem, because her child would be conceived by the Holy Spirit. (More about that on December 20) Soon after, Mary left Nazareth to stay with Cousin Elizabeth, probably to share the comfort and support of her older cousin and possibly to hide from the gossip in Nazareth about an unmarried teenager getting pregnant. As the story goes, when they saw each other, the child in Elizabeth's womb jumped in recognition, and Elizabeth was filled with the Holy Spirit. The child that was to be named John, meaning "Jehovah is gracious," was the first to recognize the One who was to be the embodied grace of God for the world. Elizabeth, uncharacteristically, blurted out, "God has blessed you above all women, and He has blessed the child you carry." And then she wondered why she was given the honor of having the mother of her Lord now come to her. If we wanted to answer her question, we might say, *Elizabeth, your very life is an oath to God, and He has chosen you to bear the second Elijah.* Then she was treated to Mary's *Magnificat*, the praise song that had been sung throughout the course of the Church's life. The two women shared their stories for three months, and then Mary returned to Nazareth.

Very soon after, Elizabeth delivered her boy. After eight days, the time for circumcision arrived. Luke says: "They [whoever "they" are] wanted to name him Zechariah, because that was his father's name." The relatives and the priests that had gathered expected and perhaps tried to insist on a traditional and proper choice of name. And without skipping a beat, Elizabeth spoke for both parents, spoke with no uncertain sound: "No, his name will be John." Then Zechariah asked for a tablet. *Ah, they think, he will override his pushy wife and announce in writing that the child will be his own namesake.* He wrote, "His name is John." Not will be—*is*. Present tense. An absolute fact. And in the claiming of it, he was freed from the consequence of his self-doubt. He spoke.

In that day, a husband's wife had the primary responsibility for raising their child. How did Elizabeth do? Well, she raised a son who had the nerve and self-confidence to pursue a very different path than his father's. He lived an unspoiled, holy and disciplined life. He became the conscience of a nation. He spoke piercing truth to power. He did all of this, and yet, as a successful adult revivalist who was famous throughout the land, he met his cousin Jesus and said to his own disciples, "Look! The Lamb of God who takes away the sin of the world!" (John 1:29, 36) At the peak of his popularity, he became Jesus' greatest promoter—an Elijah, now identifying who the Messiah actually was. So, how do you think Elizabeth did as a mother to prepare John to be the forerunner of Jesus?

Jesus' mission was to save and change the world. John's was to prepare the way. Believing Elizabeth did more than her fair share to make that possible.

Prayer

Thank you, Lord, for the confidence You have in us to be and do what we rightfully don't have the confidence to believe we can be and do on our own. I ask You to give me Elizabeth's quiet faith in Your sufficiency to bring about change in my life and to use me to be a part of Your mission to change the world. Give me faith beyond my own ability and power beyond my own weakness. I pray this through our Lord Jesus, who is more than worthy of my total trust. Amen.

DECEMBER 13

Recognizing: Seeing Change

Scripture—Luke 2:21-35

A few Advents ago, when our grandson Will was about three, I told him we would soon be celebrating the birth of Jesus. After giving me a puzzled look, he said, "I thought Jesus was born *last* Christmas. Is He going to be born again?"

Good question. Hopefully, He *will* be born again this year and every year of our lives. This Advent season is about Jesus showing up—the same Person but in a new way for our lives and for our time. He always has something new to show us, tell us, teach us. Even more importantly, He wants to reveal something else about Himself we didn't know before or weren't ready to see or receive. Yes, Will, Jesus needs to be born again in some *new* way for each of us. The question is: Will we be there when He shows up? And will we recognize Him?

Luke tells the story of Mary and Joseph presenting their baby Jesus in the temple for circumcision and having Him named by a priest eight days after the birth. Then at forty days, they bring the child again to the temple for the ritual cleansing. For the ritual sacrifice, they can only afford the poor man's offering—a pair of turtledoves or young pigeons. A man named Simeon is also on his way to the temple. We aren't told who he is. He could be a prophet or perhaps a rabbi. Luke describes him as "righteous and devout," a man eagerly anticipating "the restoration of Israel," a man on whom the Holy Spirit rests. The Spirit has now revealed to him that he won't die before he has seen "the Lord's Christ [the Anointed One, the Messiah]."

Led by the Spirit, Simeon entered the temple. Maybe he was thinking that day would be the day of Miracle. He saw Mary and Joseph and their forty-day-old child, and something told him—perhaps the Spirit—to take Jesus in his arms. He asked these parents of meager means if he could hold their child. Perhaps the baby cried as babies often do when handed over to the arms of a stranger, and maybe Simeon had to rock him for a minute or two to calm him down. Perhaps the child didn't stop crying at all until he was handed back to His mother. Either way, whether the child was quiet or vocal, Simeon looked down at Him and was sure of what he saw: He saw God's future. Through this child, everything would change. Simeon saw the long-awaited salvation—for "all people"—"a light for revelation to the Gentiles [all non-Jews] and a glory for [God's] people Israel [all Jews]." For everyone. In the bundle in his arms, Simeon recognized what he and all Israel were waiting for. This child is the Child who would change the world.

Why was Simeon chosen by God to see "the Lord's Christ" when the one he saw was only a fragile infant? Others were given this privilege before Simeon: Joseph, Mary, common shepherds, Magi from the East—to mention only those we know about. So why was Simeon given the privilege, and why was his story included by Luke? Perhaps it is because we have something to learn from Simeon. Perhaps he can teach us how to recognize Jesus ourselves.

The story gives us clues. It teaches us that there are ways we can improve our spiritual vision. We can, like Simeon, believe the promises of God so much that we actually start and continue living as if they were already in the process of being fulfilled. Simeon lived a life of righteousness and devotion. By doing so, he put himself in a better position to recognize Jesus. We are in an even more advantageous position. We can live the life the adult Jesus actually taught us to live in the Gospels, giving us a vantage point better to recognize His presence in our world. When we live Jesus better, we see Jesus better. If you want to see Jesus in a fresh and challenging way this Advent season, live His life as you have never lived it before.

There is another clue this story of Simeon gives us about recognizing Jesus in the world. We can learn to worship, not just attend worship. Luke says the Holy Spirit guided Simeon into the temple. He came and he worshiped in expectation. He opened his heart to the voice of God. Never mind that the voice was the cry of an infant. He heard it as the voice of God arriving in the flesh of helpless infancy, born into poverty and never to leave it, crowned as Lord on the Cross of execution, raised from death to give us life eternal and to send His Spirit to guide and empower us as His radical disciples. This is the Jesus who, along with the Father and the Spirit, we worship. This is the Jesus who will come again this season to reveal Himself and be worshiped by those who are ready to see Him for who He really is and not what they want to make Him.

When we see Jesus—truly see Him—we will see change. We will see salvation now offered "in the presence of all people," Jews and Gentiles alike. And as with Simeon, it will overflow into a song (vss. 29-32). The words of the song will cause us to look at our narrow Christianity and to ask the Lord to show us how we need to expand the boundaries of our gospel. The other thing we will see, says Simeon, is Jesus causing an upheaval—a sign generating opposition, the revealing of our private and inner thoughts (vss. 34-35a). These words are spoken specifically to Mary, for she will live to see her Son crucified, and the cruel piercings of His death will penetrate her own heart (v. 35b). To see Jesus is to open ourselves to the judgment of His death. He becomes the Messiah despised and rejected by humans like us, tortured for loving us beyond measure, put to death for our salvation.

If we are to recognize Jesus for who he is this Advent, we must recognize change. A change from our settled Christianity to a courageous Christian faith that follows a suffering Messiah into the world. A change from our compromised living to an unsettled Salvationism. A change from safe huddles with fellow Christians to outrageously inclusive corps congregations.

This Advent season, do as Simeon did: take the Christ Child in your arms. Observe His vulnerability, and remember that He never surrendered that vulnerability, all the way to the Cross.

Are you ready to embrace the Child in your arms and follow where His life leads you?

Prayer

Discerning Lord, give me the vision to see Jesus as He really is and not as I want to re-make Him for my comfort and satisfaction. Help me to appreciate and accept the Gospel's wooing and prodding of me toward a better likeness to Him. And please give me the fiber and strength to change my ways better to resemble Him. I ask this in His holy name. Amen.

December 14

Preparing: Getting Ourselves in Shape for Change

Scripture—Luke 2:36-38

Paired with and within the story of Simeon's encounter with the Holy Family in the temple is the story of Anna. The paragraph about her tells us that she was the daughter of Phanuel, who belonged to the tribe of Asher. In the Old Testament, we learn that Asher was the twelfth son of Jacob and an ancestor of one of the twelve tribes. We are not told the name of Anna's husband, probably because he had died in the seventh year of their marriage, and since Deborah was now eighty-four years old. The marriage had probably taken place when she was a teenager, which resulted in her living the great majority of her life without him.

So what had Anna been doing all those decades of her widowhood? Luke gave her the title of *prophetess*—a rare title for a Jewish woman in Jesus' day. It wasn't quite as rare in the Old Testament. Moses' sister Miriam was a prophetess who grabbed a tambourine and led the Israelite ladies in a celebration dance after God rescued His people from Pharaoh and his army (Exodus 15:20-21). Deborah was described as a prophetess and leader whose prophetic insights were used to settle disputes and whose strategic brilliance and heroic actions were the key to the defeat of King Jabin of Canaan (Judges 4:4-24). And as if she hadn't done enough already, she composed and sang the poetry of their victory (chapter 5). Huldah was another prophetess—a contemporary of Jeremiah. It was she who delivered the prophecy that drove King Josiah to the temple to rediscover the words of the covenant and the law, thereby lighting the fire of a spiritual reformation (II Kings 22:14-20; 23:1-25). And just as there were false prophets, there were also false prophetesses, including Noadiah, an adversary of Nehemiah (Nehemiah 6:14).

When we come to the New Testament, at Pentecost, the apostle Peter quoted a prophecy from Joel that, in the last days, God would pour out His Spirit on all people. The first manifestation of this outpouring would be that Israel's daughters, as well as their sons, would prophesy, their young would see visions, and their elders would dream dreams (Acts 2:16-17). Years later, mention is made of Philip having four daughters who were involved in the work of prophecy (Acts 21:9), but no further mention is made of them. Anna is singled out as the one prophetess in the New Testament who plays a significant role in the gospel story.

Prophets and prophetesses channel the divine. They are spokespersons for God. Their gift is to see, hear and discern what others don't or won't. They see the unseeable, discern the unknowable and trust the unbelievable. Their gift, however, is not received with ease. Anna is the perfect example. She was constant in the temple, faithfully worshipping, fasting, and praying night and day. Like Simeon, she also was given the promise that the Messiah would arrive in her lifetime. As she approached Simeon and the Holy Family, her heart was racing, her mind was open, her prophetic spirit was dancing in anticipation. This was the moment that would fulfill her hope and define her life. Anna, whose very name means "grace," was about to behold the infancy of grace in all its fullness.

How did Anna know this Child was the long-awaited Messiah, the Liberator of her people, the Redeemer of Israel? She knew, because she was prepared to know. She had been living her life to this end. In a very real sense, she had been living in such positive expectation that it was almost as if the Messiah had already come—or as New Testament scholar G. B. Caird put it, she was "agog for the coming of the gospel." Her hope showed all over her.

If you and I are to be prepared to receive the gift of Jesus anew this Advent season, like Anna we will need to live in preparation. We can nurture our hunger for Christ, not through the traditional overindulgences of this season, but by carving out time for seeking prayer and perhaps even a fasting of some kind. We can go often to church to be caught up in the Scripture, the music, the public prayer, the sermons of expectation and the fellowship of fellow waiters. We can look into the faces of those we most love, those we work and fellowship with, and especially those who live in poverty and pain, and in these faces see the face of Jesus newly revealed. We can look into our own souls, confess the sins that block our spiritual vision and vitality, and prepare ourselves to receive the living Christ in a new way.

During an Advent season many years ago, when our daughter Holly was a small child, I asked her if she was looking forward to Christmas. She assured me she was. I then asked her what her favorite thing about Christmas was. Answering in a tone that conveyed incredulity that I would ask a question to which the answer was so obvious, she replied, "Daddy! Getting presents, *of course*."

Holly was right. We all are looking forward to presents. Presents come in many forms, but they all come from someone. What shapes the value of any present is who the giver is and why the gift is given. The real present is the giver, and the real treasure is the very presence of the giver that the present evokes in us.

This Advent season, let us look for Jesus to be present with us in a new, even life-transforming way. Let us not so much seek the gifts He may give us as the company He will keep with us. Our present is His presence.

Perhaps you would like to turn the verse of a well-known Christmas carol (SBSA, 118, v. 3) into your personal prayer:

O holy Child of Bethlehem, descend to me I pray;
Cast out my sin and enter in, be born in me today.
I hear the Christmas angels the great glad tidings tell;
O come to me, abide with me, my Lord Immanuel.
Amen.

PS—And, by the way, don't forget what happened as soon as Anna encountered the Child. "She . . . began to praise God and speak about Jesus to everyone who was looking forward to the redemption of Israel." In our day and in our way, we are called to go and do likewise!

DECEMBER 15

Confessing: Starting Over

Scripture—Luke 3:3, 10-14

Advent is about preparing to receive Christ into our lives in a new way, as the prayer verse in yesterday's meditation suggests. This invasion of Christ always asks of us some change. For the follower of Jesus, the change typically requires the removal of something that doesn't conform to Jesus' likeness and the addition of what does.

I well remember something that happened at one of our family dinners when I was a teenager. Surprisingly, the biscuits my mother served that evening were just plain awful. An unspoken rule in the family was that we never criticized Mother's cooking. But that night, there was tension in the air, because, well, we were appalled at the taste. Finally, one of us children (who will not be named) blurted out that these were the strangest biscuits he (or she) had ever eaten. This was immediately followed by the stern stare of our father at the sibling who dared to demean Mother's baking. Mother, however, was already trying to solve the mystery. "Phil," she asked, "are you sure you got the right thing when I sent you next door to borrow some baking powder?" "Baking *powder?*" I asked sheepishly. "I think I asked for baking *soda.*"

During this Advent season, we are invited to remove something in our lives that is unworthy of a follower of Jesus and replace it with something that is. In case you are surprised to hear the purpose of the Advent season described in a way so similar to how we describe the purpose of the Lenten season leading up to Good Friday and Easter, the Advent season leading up to Christmas was originally established as a shorter Lenten season—a time for self-assessment and prayer in preparation for receiving the Incarnate Christ come Christmas. The first step in this process is what we call confession. Confession is the admission that something wrong or defective in our lives needs changing. As followers of Jesus, we can approach the Father through Jesus to confess our sins and receive forgiveness and cleansing (I John 1:9). Recognizing that our sins almost always affect our relationships, James invites us also to confess our sins to each other (James 5:16). We are a part of each other's healing. This is especially true when our sin has harmed a specific person, to whom we simply must go in humility and confess. Even after doing so, sometimes we must live with the person's refusal to forgive us. We still honor that person, however, whereas before we had dishonored him or her.

Christian confession does not stop with the confessing. It is followed by the determination to replace the wrong or defect with something that is a genuine creation of Christ. The change we seek is more fully to acquire the character and compassion of Christ. We not only own our sin and shortcomings; we begin the process of changing toward His likeness. John the Baptist, Jesus' forerunner, helped begin the revival in Judea by preaching to large crowds that they needed to confess their sins and receive God's forgiveness. He used a traditional practice of water baptism to help people mark and remember their confessions. Those who were baptized, however, were not left without some very basic guidelines for how they were to live differently. Whoever had two shirts was to share one with the person who had none. The same was true for one's food supply. Tax collectors, who typically kept back from their collections more than they were authorized to, were told not to take any more than the legally set percentage. Soldiers were told not to cheat or harass anyone and to be satisfied with their pay. This was to prepare the way for Jesus the Messiah, who would spell out in far more detail an even more exceptional and radical way to live.

The whole point of confessing and receiving God's forgiveness is to clear the way and empower us to live the life of Jesus. Some see confessing as getting off scot-free, receiving another excuse slip for sinning. True confessing is starting over. Some of us need to start our whole lives over again—so far have we strayed from God. Others of us who have been on this journey with Jesus realize that there are some ingredients still needed in the mix of our lives that will bring us closer to likeness to Jesus. Whichever description fits us, there is a starting over to which Jesus calls us. If we confess without making a new start, our confession—no matter how emotionally high-powered—is empty.

Beginning again is God's gift to us. He gives us a night of renewing sleep every twenty-four hours so we can start over refreshed the next day. He even gives us the freedom to fail, to learn from our failure, and then to try again, a little (or a lot) wiser. He gives us the grace to admit our mistakes and confess our sins, and the freedom to try again. That's why the Bible's insistence on not hiding our failures is good news. We can confess and start over.

The Jesus of the Gospels never meets a person He doesn't believe can start over. At the top of that list are those who are sinners and know it; at the bottom (but still on the list!) are the self-righteous who find it so very hard to admit they are sinners. If you are a seeker after God and His forgiveness, you need have no worry over your qualifications. You can start over forgiven and begin your journey with Jesus. If you are now a follower of Jesus and His Holy

Spirit has revealed to you that there is an ingredient in your living that detracts from the taste and character of your life, the Holy Spirit will give you the ingredient of Christ. It does us no good to sit around the dinner table of our church family and pretend that there are no inferior or wrong ingredients in our lives—not that we are called to condemn one another. We are called to be a community of forgiveness and grace, a place where we can start over and change, in the presence and love of Christ. This is what the true Church of Jesus looks like.

Could there be a better way, a better preparation, for welcoming the Christ into our midst this Christmas?

Prayer

Living Lord, I bring my imperfections to You this Advent season, and I ask Your Holy Spirit to show me how I can discover completeness in Christ. I confess my sins against You, and I ask Your forgiveness; and if I have hurt or sinned against other persons, I ask that You humble me before them. If I have been guilty of the self-righteousness that You so much deplore, help me to see myself through lenses that are clear of my obscuring pride, so that I can truly confess and start over. And if there is any ingredient in my life that is unholy or inconsistent with Christ, please show me, forgive me, and change my heart so that I can change my living.

I pray this through Jesus Christ, my Lord and my Life Model. Amen.

DECEMBER 16

Progressing: Living Life Forward

Scripture—Romans 13:11-14

In 2000, a movie called *Pay It Forward* hit the theaters and became very popular. It was about Trevor, a twelve-year-old boy with an alcoholic mother. His social studies teacher gave each student in the class an assignment to come up with a plan to make the world better. Trevor came up with the idea that one person should do a needed favor for three people who could not do it for themselves. Each of those three people would then need to do a favor for three other people—creating over a relatively short period of time an explosion of goodwill.

I mention the movie, because it has hints of our calling as followers of Jesus to *live life forward*. God came into the world in the Person of Jesus. (We call this, by the way, the First Advent or coming of Jesus.) Jesus started a movement, reached thousands, was crucified and rose from the dead. He did not, however, suddenly make the world a better place. He left a band of Holy-Spirit-filled disciples who were empowered to live out and spread the news of a Kingdom of God that would one day come in its fullness. (We call this the Second Advent.) In the meantime, however, these disciples were to go about living in total allegiance to their Lord Jesus and making the values of God's Kingdom of compassion their absolute guidebook, as crazy as it made them appear in a world that saw and did things differently. They were to live forward as beacon lights of God's future. They were to live every day as if the Kingdom of God were on the horizon and they were on the edge of it.

We have no basis to conclude almost two thousand years later that the plan has now changed. What has changed is that over the years, it was put away for safekeeping by most Christians, who saw their Christianity as a kind of eternity-time club membership, not a call to radical Kingdom-of-God living and action in the here and now.

In the Scripture passage named at the start of this chapter, the apostle Paul gives a clarion wake-up call to the Church in Rome. He senses the Kingdom on the horizon:

> Now our salvation is nearer than when we first had faith. The night is almost over, and the day is near. So let's get rid of the actions that belong to the darkness and put on the weapons of light. Let's behave appropriately as people who live in the day . . . .

Here we are almost twenty centuries later, and still, we live on the expectant edge. Spectacular forecasters of End Times always fail with their settings of the exact year or dates. It is curious that they continue their speculations in spite of Jesus' statement that no one, not even Jesus Himself, knows the day or hour. There seems to be a very good purpose to this unpredictability: to keep us alert and living by the values of God's Kingdom so that whenever Jesus returns, we are ready (Mark 13:32-37).

Paul does not give the Church in Rome a comprehensive list of dos and don'ts for this way of living. His list is probably illustrative or suggestive of a broader list, or it may address some specific concerns Paul has about this particular church, especially since it is located in the capital of the powerful Roman Empire. Whatever the context of that place and time, the admonitions speak to us all. First, he says, *open your eyes and arm yourself with the weapons of light. Live in the light of day and not in the scandals of darkness. Second, so dress yourself with Jesus that your identity and lifestyle are clear. And third, don't make any plans involving the indulgence of your selfish desires and motivations.* He is urging others to live in the Kingdom of God, whose values are very different from those of the Roman Empire. It is therefore revolutionary, sometimes even seditious. Over the years, many faithful Christians have paid a steep price, including the ultimate price, for living in God's Kingdom.

The fact is that in some real way, Jesus is coming today, and tomorrow, and the next day, and every day. Remember when He was leaving after the first visit, He said He would send the Holy Spirit. In other words, Jesus visits us every day through His Spirit! We need to be looking for Him everywhere. We need to be living the way He shows us. We need to be ready for His coming at any time.

Os Guinness tells the story of something that happened about 250 years ago in the Connecticut House of Representatives. The House was in session on a bright day in May, and the delegates were about to do their work by natural light. But then something happened that no one expected. Right in the middle of debate, there was an eclipse of the sun, and everything turned to darkness. Some legislatures thought it was the Second Coming. So, a clamor arose. People wanted to adjourn. People wanted to pray. People wanted to prepare for the coming of the Lord.

The speaker of the House, however, had a different idea. He was a Christian believer, and he rose to the occasion with good logic and good faith. "We are all upset by this strange darkness," he said, "and some of us are afraid. But the Day of the Lord is either approaching or it is not. If it is not, there is no cause for adjournment. And if the Lord is returning, I, for one, choose to be found doing my duty. I therefore ask that the candles be brought." And men who expected Jesus went back to their desks and resumed their debate. (Recounted in "Between Two Advents: In the Interim," Cornelius Plantinga, Jr., *Christian Century*, Dec. 6, 2000, p. 1,272.)

The speaker of the House knew what it meant to live in readiness for the coming of God's Kingdom in fullness. It did not mean a mad dash to get ready for Jesus' arrival. It meant to live every day in readiness. We can call it living life forward, in the presence of Jesus, who is with us today and will one day bring us to the Kingdom of His family forever.

Prayer

Dear Lord, forgive me for the times I have failed to see You, failed to obey You, failed to be like You. Thank You for staying with me in spite of my negligence and distractedness. Please help me in my living each day to imbibe the motivation of Your heart and to follow the course of Your life away from recognition and toward compassionate service. And in doing so, may I live every day forward toward the full realization of Your Kingdom. I offer this prayer in the name of my ever-present Lord, Jesus Christ. Amen.

DECEMBER 17

HUMBLING: GETTING DOWN TO EARTH

Scripture—Philippians 2:1-11

I like to sing in the shower. Do you? You may otherwise be very timid about your vocal cords. Perhaps on Sunday morning, you sing with great reserve. The shower or bathtub is a different matter. It is the place where all of us can be liberated to cut loose with unrepressed melodies and fill the world with music—even if that world is only the bathroom.

After all, don't I sound good in the shower? For those fleeting moments, in a small room that makes my voice seem big, with tiled walls that bounce and amplify the sound and mist-laden air that adds body and richness to each sung note, I sound like...well, Pavarotti.

Don't we all prefer to place ourselves in settings where we come off sounding or looking good? For that matter, don't we like to be around people who feed our egos? Is it even possible that we have a favorite little mutual admiration society at church, or at work, or somewhere—some cozy group in which the adulation of our allies stretches the truth about us ridiculously thin? If we like to hang out in such agreeable groups, we may find it increasingly difficult to be around people who disagree with us. And we may really find it difficult to be around people we secretly suspect may see a side of us we try hard to hide—people who might even speak truth to us. Our self-pride can be terribly fragile.

The apostle Paul wrote a letter to the church in Rome—a congregation he didn't know well. So, he wrote in a more general, broadly applicable way. In addressing the danger of spiritual pride, he pled with every member to avoid this insidious malady: "... don't think of yourself more highly than you ought to think" (Romans 12:3b). No Christian is immune to the temptation to spiritual pride. No saint is beyond susceptibility to the creeping invasion of spiritual self-delusion. None of us is forever removed from the possibility of inflated opinions about ourselves. "So those who think they are standing need to watch out or else they may fall" (I Cor. 10:12).

Setting limits to our pretensions and delusions about ourselves must be one of the hardest things for us to do. Society teaches us to look upon ourselves, and try to have others look upon us, in ways that are personally advantageous. We give in to this temptation by pursuing measures of success that may be a mile wide but only an inch deep. Even ministers of the Gospel are often judged on how they stack up against their colleagues in size of membership and budget. By the same token, a corps can be lured into a culture of artificial growth by making itself more attractive with programs that keep people busy but unengaged on a deeper level—people who are happy but overly cautious about upsetting the apple cart. So, they keep their opinions to themselves or only express ideas that are acceptable on the whole.

And then something happens that upsets this whole order. Someone expresses an opinion that is contrary, and others don't know how to handle it. It doesn't take long for arguments to multiply and tensions and tempers to rise. This seemed to have begun to happen in the Philippian church, a congregation Paul knew well. Paul loved this congregation, and they loved him. They were well along in their spiritual journey. Paul heard, however, that some differences of opinion had arisen between Euodia and Syntyche, both of whom had been important partners in the Gospel with

Paul. It is likely that other people had become confused or had taken sides. (Philippians 4:2-3)

Is this indicative of some spiritual problem in the Philippian congregation—or in any congregation, for that matter? Not necessarily. Differences arise in any congregation, because God did not make us all the same (Thank heavens!). Our personalities differ, and we think differently. To be honest, some differences do attach themselves to self-serving, scheming and other sinful motives. The challenge for a corps congregation is to invalidate unworthy motives and find a resolution that honors and incorporates the differences. Unity is always strengthened by the celebration and employment—and where needed, the resolution—of our differences.

This is easier said than done. Perhaps we've seen corps conflicts divide a corps too often. What does Paul have to say about that? What's the solution when disagreements become testy or hungry egos go on a feeding frenzy to satisfy a need for recognition and self-esteem? Paul's answer is one of the most eloquent and powerful statements in Scripture. It begins with: "Adopt the attitude that was in Christ Jesus" (Phil. 2:5). This is followed with a beautiful and poignant summation of the Gospel story from the divine Son's self-emptying to become one of us, to His voluntary suffering and death for our salvation, and finally to His resurrection and exaltation by the heavenly Father (Read vv. 6-11.). Paul is saying to the Philippian church and to us all: *As your very salvation derives from the compassion of our self-emptying God, so you have life together as the very Body of Christ only when your corps throbs with the spirit of this self-emptying humility.*

A corps with an assortment of different personalities and opinions, and even with unworthy motives on the part of some members, will begin to move toward authentic unity only as compassionate disciples of one loving Lord. The evidence is when members begin to humble themselves before Christ and one another. This does not mean considering oneself of no value, making oneself a doormat to be stepped on and abused. It is rather a humility of spirit, a willingness to consider the other person as if he were better than yourself. It means a willingness to defer to a brother or sister, to put ourselves in their place. It means getting down to the lowliness of the earth from which we were created, emptying ourselves of pride and any need to defend or justify ourselves. It means having the mind of our self-lowering Christ.

Are you willing to lead the way in your corps? As you prepare to receive the humble Christ Child anew this Christmas, there is no better way than to humble yourself, to rid yourself of your pretensions so as to receive the Child who lowered Himself and gave up His rightful claims in order to bring us back to God. You may even start a movement.

Prayer

Dear humbling Lord, teach me that I am Your child, Your disciple, Your servant—and to see these as my only glory. Show me the utter futility of fighting for position or power, of defending myself when there is no need, of arguing for a point that is finally pointless, and of refusing to concede when nothing is to be gained by persisting. Please keep showing me how to humble myself before others while not compromising Your Gospel or Your way of holiness. And in particular, I ask that You help me live this way, starting this very day. I pray this in the name of my exalted Lord, the Christ of the lowly human road. Amen.

"... the one who is to be born will be holy. He will be called God's Son" (Luke 1:35b).

WEEK FOUR
WAITING FOR THE MIRACLE

DECEMBER 18

Foretelling Angel

Scripture—Luke 1:26-33

Our doubts and fears are perhaps the influences that most paralyze us. They are the perfect crippling combination. They feed on each other. They sap our energy. Together they are lethal to the spirit. William Shakespeare was right:

> Our doubts are traitors and make us lose the good we oft might win, by fearing to attempt.
>
> (*Measure for Measure*, Act 1, Scene 4)

These are not doubts that cause us to question ideas and things. God gave us brains to be able to do that and make wise decisions. The doubts that disable us are of the spirit. We doubt God, and in doubting God, we doubt ourselves. Perhaps it works the other way as well. If we have deep doubts about ourselves, we may transfer that doubt to the God who created us, as if He were responsible for our lack of faith.

What do you do when an angel appears to you? Like most of us, you probably haven't had that experience. But if you did, what would you do? Once you got over the shock, you'd probably listen to him or her. Well, what might that angel say? Interesting question. Let the Bible be our guide.

In the Old Testament, the Lord spoke to His people either through an angel or prophetic figure, or sometimes directly. On most of those occasions, two things would be said. One was that

God was about to do something big, either by Himself or through them. The other was an assuring command: "Don't be afraid!" In the New Testament, angel appearances are especially associated with events relating to Jesus. The angel Gabriel appeared individually to Zechariah, Mary and Joseph. Zechariah was told that he and his wife, Elizabeth, would have a son called John, forerunner to Jesus. Mary and Joseph were told separately that they would have a son called Jesus. All three were assured there was nothing of which they should be afraid. Many years later, Jesus Himself was praying in a garden, seeking the courage to face His cruel, torturous death, and a God-sent angel came to His side and strengthened Him, as he helped Him not to be governed by His fear. And finally, when God's future was soon to be consummated, the angel appeared in Revelation to reveal "the river of life-giving water, shining like crystal, flowing from the throne of God and the Lamb . . . the tree of life . . . for the healing of the nations . . ."—the Kingdom's full consummation. The curse of sin was gone, and all barriers to the worship of God were removed. There was no more fear.

Still, we live with our fears and doubts. We all have them. The question for us is whether or not we will allow them to control us. To live with the terrifying thought that the worst will happen renders us weak and helpless. To live doubting God's enabling power and our ability to do what He may be asking of us is to doubt ourselves. When President Franklin Roosevelt used his first inaugural address to speak to a nation that was in the midst of the Great Depression, he knew that people were worried about America's future. Life was unsettled, and things would never be quite the same again. Roosevelt knew the disabling power of fear and knew it brought out the worst in people. Confident in the emerging strength of this great nation and its democracy, he declared war on fear as he uttered those memorable words: " ... the only thing we have to fear is fear itself."

It is amazing how those words spoken for political purposes perfectly state what we Christians must deal with as we confront what God is asking of us. God, it seems, usually asks of us something we do not find easy to do. Otherwise, we would do it naturally, without being asked. Why else would His angels and prophets start off with "Don't be afraid?" They know that being on a mission from God carries risk, whether that risk is the possibility of embarrassing failure or some level of opposition or even suffering.

An angel named Gabriel appeared to a teenage girl in an obscure town in Galilee called Nazareth. She was pledged to be married to a carpenter named Joseph sometime in the future. But Gabriel seemed to be rushing things. The marriage hadn't even taken place yet; it probably hadn't even been scheduled. "Don't be afraid," said Gabriel. "Here's what will happen. You will conceive and bear a Son, and the name you will give Him is Jesus. He will be so great that He will be called 'the Son of the Most High.' He'll be granted 'the throne of David His Father.' He'll be ruler over Jacob's house forever, and His Kingdom will have no end."

Can you imagine what this teenager from a little cow town like Nazareth, married to a carpenter of very humble estate, thought about this astounding message? I don't think the angel's visit was as short as it seems in the text, nor that the message he gave was as rapid-fire as the words appear in Luke. I imagine Gabriel would have given Mary time to take in each of the statements and would have explained what they meant in a little more detail. (As the Gospels do not record everything said in connection with Jesus' birth, life and ministry over the almost four years, it is quite possible that Gabriel said more on this visitation.) I can also imagine that Mary was stunned and overwhelmed by what she heard. I imagine that Gabriel waited patiently for her to begin to receive it.

Mary must have wondered why she, a poor teenager from the sticks, would be called to play such a crucial role in God's messianic plans. The whole idea must have scared her. How was she able to overcome her sense of inadequacy and her fears? I suggest it was the plain and simple fact that she loved God with all her heart. Her love overcame her fear, just as the evangelist John said in his first letter: "Perfect love drives out fear" (I John 4:18b). It is fear that opposes love. It is fear that blocks our loving. When someone we deeply love asks us to do something that takes us out of our comfort zone, we do it. We give in to love.

As we now prepare ourselves to receive the Christ again at Christmastime, let us release our love for our Lord in worship and adoration. We will then be better prepared for what the Incarnate Christ may ask of us who love Him, this season and for the rest of our lives. We may even be prepared for a miracle.

Prayer

Dear God, like Mary I stand before You in awe and wonder that You chose me to carry the love of Your Son and our Christ into the world. You have given me more than enough reasons to love You, so much so that whatever fear I have has no real power to stop my witness and compromise my living. Help me to live beyond my fear each day, so that I will, like Mary, receive the calling You give me and pursue it with all my love. I ask this in the name of the Christ whom I even now prepare myself to receive and embrace anew this Christmas season. Amen.

DECEMBER 19

Confused and Righteous Joseph

Scripture—Matthew 1:18-25

Joseph, the carpenter and husband-to-be of Mary, is one of the most interesting figures in the story of Jesus' Nativity. We meet him first in Matthew's Gospel. Gabriel appeared to him after it had become obvious that Mary, to whom he had been engaged, was pregnant. To put it mildly, Joseph was confused, especially since they had been very careful not to have sex during the engagement. We aren't told whether or not Mary shared her earlier encounter with Gabriel where she was informed that she would conceive a son by the Holy Spirit. If she shared that encounter, can you imagine this carpenter, whose world consisted mostly of palpable things like hammers and wood, trying to get his mind around a child being conceived by Spirit? Nothing like this had ever happened. It seemed more likely Mary did not share the visitation from Gabriel. Joseph would have been deeply hurt by the pregnancy and shocked that his beloved fiancée had acted sinfully and violated their engagement.

I was intrigued to learn something interesting about early depictions of the Nativity in the Orthodox Christian Church. In the West, we are used to Nativity paintings of the Baby Jesus, Mary and Joseph at the center, surrounded by shepherds, sometimes Magi (though they actually came later), various animals and angels hovering above. Many of the early Orthodox paintings, however, placed Joseph outside the stable or cave, somewhere either below or off to the side. He is sitting on a rock, his head resting on his right hand, looking very confused. Nearby there is sometimes an old hermit looking down into Joseph's face, as if he were trying to help Joseph through the crisis. Paintings often compress time, and it may be that the confused Joseph was the earlier Joseph still trying to figure it all out. Frankly, it's worth being reminded that these events were a little messier than we sometimes try to depict them in our rush to make God's dealings with us look so piously perfect. They usually aren't.

Lord knows we who are fathers manage to feel helpless enough when it comes to knowing the right things to do when our children are born. Joseph's depiction as concerned and confused is a touch of honesty. Good fathers are concerned about being able to provide for their children. Here was Joseph, having been told that their son will be called "God-with-us" (Emmanuel), here to "save His people from their sins." What was Joseph able to provide for this Savior Jesus' birthing? Only a smelly stable! What kind of a father is that? Maybe a father we can understand.

We don't hear much more about Joseph after the birth of Jesus. He and Mary took Jesus to the Temple for His circumcision, naming and presentation. A short time later, an angel again appeared to Joseph, this time in a dream, and told him that Herod's slaughter of the infants would soon take place. He directed Joseph to take Mary and the Child and flee to Egypt for safety. Joseph immediately obeyed, thus saving Jesus' life. Joseph had undoubtedly never been to Egypt, but he went, and the rest is salvation history. After returning home to Nazareth when it was safe, he settled into his carpenter's trade, and he and Mary started raising a family. (Other children did come along!)

The next and last time we hear of Joseph is on that famous journey to Jerusalem for the Passover Festival, when Jesus was twelve.

This turned out to be a significant event in the life of Jesus. On this occasion in Jesus' life, He found His way to the temple and began listening to the teachers, putting questions to them, and then answering them in a way that demonstrated unusually profound understanding. The problem was that this was the day His parents' caravan was leaving, and Mary and Joseph assumed that He was elsewhere in the caravan. When they finally discovered He wasn't, it took three days for them to retrace their steps and finally find Him in the temple. They chastised Him, and in an act so reminiscent of beginning adolescent rebellion, Jesus reminded them that He needed to pursue what His own life was about. Luke only records what Mary said to Him in reprimand. Joseph said nothing of which we know. In fact, no Gospel writer records what Joseph actually said on any occasion.

Our righteousness isn't most measured by what we say. It's measured by how we live. Joseph was in a tough place when he realized the woman he was engaged to was pregnant, and he was not the father. What was he to do? He had the right to publicly divorce her and save his reputation, but he did not. He married her, thereby sharing her "blame." Joseph, said Matthew, was "a righteous man." Was this the beginning of a new righteousness, which placed the far greater emphasis on standing alongside, in this case even marrying, the one who was shamed? Was this a holiness defined not by sterile separation, but by up-close mercy and sacrificial love—an engaged, in-the-world holiness? I think so. Don't you?

Joseph could not be better described than in these words of William H. Willimon:

Joseph's righteousness... was so quiet. He didn't show off his righteousness at Mary's expense. How different was Joseph—wanting to do the right thing but also not wanting to harm Mary—from our image of the righteous prophet, publicly denouncing everyone else's materialism, sexism, sin.

In fact, Joseph never denounces or pronounces; he never even speaks. Mary sings, as do old Elizabeth and Zechariah, and we love and remember these jubilantly righteous people and sing their songs as Christmas carols. But Joseph the carpenter left us no poetry to sing, no dramatic scenes to depict on Christmas cards, no moving speeches about liberation of captives or light to those in darkness... His witness is that he does more than he says. He obeys the divine summons to marry, to flee to Egypt with his family, and then to return and settle in Nazareth. All without a word. His speech consists of active response to the will of God.

(*The Christian Century*, Nov. 23, 1988, pp. 1,063-1,064.)

We have none of Joseph's words to remember, but we do have his acts of righteousness. They are glimpses into his holy heart. He reminds me of some quiet Christians I know and have known who have little to say and much to show us. Like Joseph they may leave behind no memorable pronouncements. They are happy to fade from the picture leaving the legacy of their obedience, their love for God and others, and their humility. There is a purity there that can't be hidden or forgotten. Jesus, under the parenting of Joseph and Mary, turned out extraordinarily well—in fact, perfect.

Perhaps, as we prepare to contemplate again the miraculous birth of our Lord this season, we can work on a miracle or two in our own lives. Maybe we can practice doing something holy, something loving that is motivated by the Holy Spirit—and say absolutely nothing about it.

Prayer
Loving Lord, I confess that sometimes I say more than is worth saying, as if the spaces of my silence always needed filling. Save me from the tyranny of words, words, words. And please give me the grace of a quiet righteousness unrecognized. I pray this through the Son, loved and nurtured by a quiet, righteous man called Joseph—our Lord Jesus Christ. Amen.

DECEMBER 20

Overwhelmed Mary

Scripture—Luke 1:34-38; 46-56

I remember so well the birth of our two children. After ten years of marriage, Keitha and I were beginning to wonder if we would ever be able to have children of our own. We were already inquiring about adoption. And then God gave us two precious girls to love and raise. Joseph and Mary's situation was quite different. They hadn't been trying at all. In fact, they weren't even married and had abstained from premarital sex. So, how in the world did they conceive Jesus?

Don't waste time trying to figure out or explain the obstetrics of the matter, says theologian Karl Barth. What is important is that human initiative is not involved. This, like many occurrences in the Bible, is a miracle. In the case of what we call the conception by the Holy Spirit, more than conception is going on. It is creation—in fact, it is a *new creation*. As the apostle Paul puts it, we who are of the race of Adam will die, but through Christ (the Second Adam), we will be made alive (I Cor. 15:22). "The first human, Adam, became a living person, and the last Adam became a spirit that gives life" (15:45). Through Christ, this new and different Adam, anyone is now able to become part of the new creation (II Cor. 5:17)!

Mary bore a Child like no other mother has ever borne. She bore a new creation. The language the angel used for the formation of Jesus in Mary's womb is the language of creation, not conception: "The Holy Spirit will come over you and the power of the Most High will overshadow you" (Luke 1:35a). The words have the feel of Genesis 1:1-2, where creation begins with a dark, formless void over which God's wind (Spirit) sweeps, and creation is underway.

In Jesus, the *new* creation was underway. Not just another birth—a new miracle of God for the whole world!

No wonder Mary was overwhelmed! (I use the word "overwhelmed," not in the sense of being overpowered or overthrown, but in the very literal sense of the word: being turned over, or turned upside down.) Gabriel turns Mary's world upside down. Her body would bear and nurture the new creation. She and her husband, Joseph, would parent, protect and teach the new creation, from birth to adulthood. And though this Jesus will see far deeper than they can see, understand far more than they can grasp, be possessed by a vision of God beyond their own imagining, and eventually move away from them to create a far bigger and more inclusive family—their parenting played a major role. Jesus was a real man who needed real parents. To dismiss or diminish Mary and Joseph's important influence and nurture is to question the very humanity of Jesus, as if He were God in human costume rather than God in flesh.

Most of us don't like to have our world turned upside down. We like predictability and stability; we like to plan for the future. Mary was probably that kind of person. I doubt she liked to sit around waiting for something to happen. She was engaged to be married to Joseph, so she was busy preparing for the wedding and for her future life with Joseph. And then Gabriel appeared. He didn't change Mary's plans; he radically reframed them.

We don't know much about Mary the mother of Jesus. None of the Gospels give her lineage, nor do they detail her immediate background. All we know we must gather from the Nativity accounts of her responses to the angelic announcement, and from the few accounts of her interaction with Jesus over the course of His ministry and of her presence as a participant of the Church in Acts.

Because of the scarcity of information about Mary, we are sorely tempted to portray her in terms that make her seem, well, perfect or even almost-beyond-human. The paintings of Mary and the Christ Child often give her an otherworldly look, accentuated by a prominent halo. In children's nativity plays, we usually choose to have Mary played by a girl who we are fairly confident will sit still and quietly look angelic. If there is a speaking part for Mary, we typically expect that she will speak with a certain pious compliance, a lack of forceful passion. This is particularly strange in light of the song she sang to Elizabeth—remember, the song about her incredulity over someone of her low estate being chosen for this mission, about God getting ready to flex His muscles and scatter the arrogant, pull the powerful down from their thrones, and relieve the rich of their wealth (Luke 1:46-55)! John Wesley commented that this passage should cause us to number Mary among the prophets—none of whom, we might add, were passive and sweet.

God seems to have a habit of choosing less-than-perfect people. You know this if you know your Bible. We will never be able to identify Mary—or identify *with* her—if we see her as God's absolutely perfect choice based on the depth and breadth of her spirituality and some spectacular track record in righteousness. Some Christians even go so far as to claim she was sinless and totally pure. We are far closer to the truth if we see her as a young teenager, still uncertain about herself and the world, engaged to and just getting to know an older man. (His older age would explain why, after the incident with twelve-year-old Jesus, he disappeared from the record. We assume that by the time Jesus began His ministry at around age thirty, Joseph has already died.) We really don't know why God chose a young woman such as Mary to bear the Messiah and become the vessel of Incarnation. What we do know is that this choice, this risk God is taking with this obscure young woman from a little known town, changed her forever. As perplexed as she was, "confused by [the angel's] words" (v. 29a), she listened to what seems so obviously to be an improbability (v. 34). She didn't dismiss the message; she sought understanding, and Gabriel told her the miracle by which it would happen. When he finished explaining, Mary said to him, "I am the Lord's servant. Let it be with me just as you have said" (v. 38). And the hovering Lord hears every word.

The question for all of us is: Do we have such a Mary in us, such a Mary as when we hear an overwhelming word from the Lord, we will pick ourselves back up off the ground, and say, "Let it be with me just as You have said"? This Advent and Christmas season, perhaps you will hear a voice or see a vision inviting you toward a calling or a task beyond what you envisioned for yourself or thought possible. Will you hear and see with a Mary-like courage? And will you act with a Mary-like faith?

Prayer
Dear God, Who loves to use lowly souls like Mary to love Yourself into the world, I offer my own unworthiness to Your desire to work through me to be a Christ-bearer in the places where I live. When I am tempted to narrow Your expectations of me, teach me that in Your hands my meagerness can be molded into a miracle of grace at work. I offer this prayer in the name of my Lord Jesus, who knows everything about me, and loves and trusts me still. Amen.

DECEMBER 21

Right Timing

Scripture—Galatians 4:4; Mark 1:14-15; Luke 12:56; Romans 5:6; 13:11-14; II Corinthians 6:2; Revelation 1:3c

Advent and Christmas are about timing—God's timing, to be exact. The apostle Paul describes the timing of Jesus' coming into the world as the fullness or fulfillment of time. That's an interesting expression. We wonder how time can come already full, like a package to be unwrapped, as if something were already there for us to discern and receive. Perhaps we will understand the Bible better if we can begin to understand this way of seeing time as well as living in time. We get a glimpse of it in Ecclesiastes 3:1-11, where there are seasons that invite us to specific activities fitting for that season. "God," the writer says, "has made everything fitting in its time..." All too often, we miss the timing. Jesus criticizes religious leaders for being able to predict the weather but not knowing what time it is. What does He mean?

In the Greek New Testament, there are two words for time. One is *chronos*, and the other is *kairos*. *Chronos* is how our world tends to see time. It has to do with the measurement of ongoing time in minutes, hours, days, months, years and eras. It is time ticking, calendar pages turning, years beginning, years ending. It is time marching by, and we are left to figure out what to do with it, how to make use of it and not waste it. We see time as empty and ourselves as the ones who are supposed to fill it with something that makes sense according to our outlook on life.

Kairos is different. It is filled rather than measured time. It is time in the hands of God. In fact, it is God's time. If we see our times as His, we are concerned with what He is up to in our days and what He wants us to be up to. If we see our times as measured units (*chronos*), we are concerned about how to fill our empty days. Obviously, we followers of Jesus must live in both these time worlds. We are not called to be so heavenly minded that we make no concrete plans, keep no appointments and accept no responsibility for the practical matters of life. We must live in the real world that runs by *chronos*. An undisciplined life, an unplanned day and a failure to take commitments seriously disable a disciple of Jesus.

The challenge for us all is to *discern the kairos in the chronos*. It is to know at any one minute or any one day, God may break in and reveal Himself in that particular minute and radically alter that particular day. The art of a Christian is to see among the commonplaces the face, voice or action of our God who is always present in one way or another, beckoning and encouraging us.

The tragedy is that we have been conditioned to see the expected normal and miss the unexpected extraordinary. I remember a story told about the Wright brothers, who had repeatedly tried to fly heavier-than-air craft. Finally, on a December day at Kitty Hawk, North Carolina, these brothers did what no other men had successfully done. They flew. Elated, they wired their sister, Katharine: "We have actually flown 120 feet! Will be home for Christmas." Katharine ran down the street and breathlessly handed the telegram to the editor of the city newspaper. He read it carefully and then smiled. "Well, well, how nice!" he said, "The boys will be home for Christmas." He missed the *kairos*—the fullness of time for the era of aviation!

I am sure that there have been the times when I was near a powerful truth, a new discovery, a new possibility for growth, a fresh opportunity—and I did not see it, or was not ready to see it. I am sure there have been many times when Christ was near, and I was not aware of Him. I was looking in my own preferred places. I was captive to the spiritual limitations and prejudices of my past. I was blind, even as my Lord was ready to open my eyes.

At this season in particular, it's worth asking if we've got our timing right. When God is ready to do something, are we able to see it and then ready to join Him? When God makes an appearance, do we show up? When God says, "Now!" do we say, "Not yet"? Almost two thousand years ago, God, who over the centuries had given His countdown through the prophets, said, "Now is the time!" The odd thing was, most of the people who should have figured it out didn't; they were looking for a messianic kingdom of personal prosperity. Some of the people who shouldn't have figured it out did; they were looking for a kingdom of God where inclusive love and righteousness reigned.

We are part of God's history moving toward fulfillment. In the world of New Testament times, history was seen by the majority as a fatalistic cycle. Everything repeated; there was finally no forward movement toward a destiny. The only hope was to be released from the vicious cycle. The Old and New Testaments speak of a God who is at work in history moving us toward His future, bringing us toward the full realization of the Kingdom of God through Jesus. To those who have given their lives to God and are following Jesus, there is no room for the boredom of every-day-the-same. Each day is unique and different, because it is one day closer to the goal to which God is bringing us. So, the way to begin every day is to ask *God* what time it is, specifically in terms of His redemptive plan for the world and His purpose for our lives in relation to it. And the way to live each day is to hear the voice of God amid all the other noises tempting us, and then to obey it.

Mark says that "Jesus came into Galilee announcing God's good news, saying, 'Now is the time! Here comes God's kingdom!'" Luke says that Jesus invites us to learn how to interpret the *kairos*. Paul tells us that at just "the right moment, Jesus died for ungodly people." He says it's time to wake up, because salvation is getting closer and closer, and we ought to start acting like it by dressing ourselves with the Lord Jesus Christ. Now is the day of salvation! And John began the last book of the New Testament by proclaiming that "the time is near." We live on the edge of eternity.

This Advent season, as we draw near to Christmas to celebrate the most perfectly timed event in the world, let's ask God to help us with our own timing. Let's ask Him to help us live in the fullness of time He's given us.

There's no point in fretting over lost time, wasted years or opportunities of which we have not taken advantage. If we want to fret, all of us have plenty to fret over. I'll match you minute for minute over God's time wasted, never grasped, lost. Instead, let's all pray, "Dear God, what time is it now for me? What is the fullness of time for me?" And then let us pray:

O Holy Child of Bethlehem, descend to us, we pray;
Cast out our sin and enter in, be born in us today.
We hear the Christmas angels the great glad tidings tell:
Oh, come to us, abide with us, our Lord Emmanuel!

And He will—because it's time.

DECEMBER 22

SUITABLE NAME

Scripture—Matthew 1:21

Joseph woke up after his dream, stunned. He tried to get his mind around it all. He'd been commanded to go ahead and take Mary as his wife, in spite of the out-of-wedlock pregnancy. He'd been told that the child Mary was carrying was not his but the Holy Spirit's. And Gabriel's final words were still ringing strongly in his ears: "She will give birth to a son, and you will call Him Jesus, because He will save His people from their sins."

The dream was over. He was man enough to go ahead and marry Mary, saving her from as much embarrassment as possible. He was trusting enough to accept on face value a concept his mind alone could not grasp: a human being conceived in a woman by the Spirit of God. That last part of the angel's announcement, however, was something he knew something about. He, an ancient Palestinian Jew, was part of a longstanding faith tradition that looked to the future for a Messiah who would come to the Jewish people and free them from their bondage. This Messiah would be their Savior

Ah, we all love a savior. There's plenty in our lives from which we'd like to be saved. We'd like to be released from any number of things that make our lives unpleasant or even miserable. Some of us may want some protection from our enemies—people who are trying to do us in. Some of us may want to be protected from failure. Some may want to be spared suffering and pain. Most of us probably wouldn't mind having our fears removed. A few of us probably wouldn't mind being rescued from parents who still want to control our lives. A few others would certainly like God to do something about their prodigal children.

The truth is this: God does not start His saving by addressing our inconveniences, frustrations and threats. He came to save us from our *sins*. That is what His name means. He came to heal our souls and correct our behavior.

Does Jesus help us deal with our enemies? Yes, He saves us from our sins so that we can see our enemies in a holy way—as no real threat. Then we can love them—which involves refusing to be their enemies and refusing to treat them as our enemies (Matthew 5:44; Luke 6:27).

Does Jesus help us deal with our failures? Yes, by forgiving our sins, He saves us from the power sin has over us. Without that demeaning power, the threat of our failures is diminished. In fact, we're freed to take risks for the right reasons, even though we know some of our attempts will fail. We couldn't do that when sin had the upper hand and gave us an arrogance that made us unable to cope with our failings. The only kind of failure Jesus prays we won't have is a failure of faith (Luke 22:32). Jesus has no problems with our other failures—only our sins.

Does Jesus help us with our suffering and pain? Yes, He saves us from our sins— driving them out with love (John 3:16). The love of God is what makes suffering bearable. "Love," says the apostle Paul, "puts up with all things, trusts in all things, hopes for all things, endures all things" (I Corinthians 13:7). God holds us in His love so that we get through all the suffering and pain we do face.

Does Jesus help us with our fears? Yes, He saves us from our sins by making our hearts vessels into which He pours His love (Romans 5:5), and this very love "drives out fear" (I John 4:18).

Does Jesus help us with our family problems? Yes, He saves us from our sins, and it is our sins that build barriers between us and divide our families. On the cross, says Paul, Jesus broke down the walls that divide us (Ephesians 2:14).

What we most need is not to be saved from our enemies, our failures, our suffering and pain, our fears, and our family problems. What we most need is surgery on our hearts—a transplant really—"a new heart," along with "a new spirit" (Ezekiel 36:26). Jesus is the giver of new hearts—healthy and pure hearts. It's our sins that give us irreparable heart damage, and Jesus *saves* us from our sins. His name is Jesus, "because He will save His people from their sins."

The name "Jesus" keeps His mission from becoming mere preaching, though those who follow Him must take His teaching seriously. It is their compass for the journey. The name "Jesus" keeps His mission from becoming a mere prescription for social change, though His Kingdom reorders our relationships and requires a keen and compassionate social conscience. The name "Jesus" keeps His mission from becoming a mere political agenda, but anyone who says it doesn't have profound political consequences hasn't read the prophets and the gospels.

Scripture reminds us of the pure hearts given to us by Jesus: "Happy are the people who have pure hearts, because they will see God" (Matthew 5:8). The heart is the well within us from which our actions are drawn. If our hearts are corrupt, the rest of us will be corrupted. Out of the heart come evil thoughts and actions (15:19), and these are what make a person unclean before God (v. 20a).

How then does God purify the heart? He applies the only medicine that can cure heart disease. Call it "God-love." At one point in His ministry, Jesus, who loves all His enemies, says to a group of them, "... I know you, that you don't have God's love in you" (John

5:42). It is this missing love that prevents the healing of the damaged heart. The heart is made for one thing only: loving God and our neighbors. Unfortunately, we all too often want to "have our cake and eat it too"—the Bible calls it a divided heart. We think and act as if we can love God and keep on loving the things and having the relationships that diminish or even destroy us. A divided heart is a dying heart. This is why we need to let God take us over, shake us up, seize our hearts as His own and recreate them with His love.

We need a new heart to enable us to love the Lord our God with all our heart (Matthew 22:37a), with a heart that's on track to do what a heart is supposed to do: pump God's love into our thinking, feeling and living, and pump it into the whole world so that we can love our neighbors as we love ourselves (19:19b). All the Law and the Prophets are fulfilled in loving God and loving our neighbors, says Jesus (22:40).

How will we know when our Lord's mission in the world is being accomplished? When He is saving His people from their sins and their "un-loving," we will know. It will begin with you and me.

Prayer

Savior Lord, reveal to me any sins of mine I am unaware of or have kept hidden, so that I may confess them and, by Your grace, cease committing them. Renew—and if need be, recreate—my heart. Save me from those thoughts and actions that do not spring from Your love [The reader may want to name them here:_____]. Please give me the will to act on this prayer, because I make it in the name of my enabling Lord—Jesus. Amen

DECEMBER 23

SPECIFIC PLACE

Scripture—Luke 2:1-7; John 1:14

In the transient and virtual world in which we now live, we are in danger of losing a sense of place. As an increasingly mobile society, many of us do not stay in one place sufficiently long enough for it to carry enduring memories of defining events in our lives. Lacking roots, we long for places that helped to define us. Further eroding our connection to specific places is the internet world which places us everywhere and in no place in particular. We can live in empty spaces which we fill with our preferred content and all too often with our illusions. The internet allows us—indeed, pressures us—to create our own world—a world hungry for "likes," pushing us into viral community. But it is a world that lives on the screen, and it tempts us away from the places where we actually live. It dis-places us.

The Bible is a book of places. It is grounded in specific places in the world where God acts and fulfills His promises, and where people interact, sin and live righteously—none of it in empty space but always grounded in locations on our planet, even if we don't know exactly where some of those places are today.

Throughout the Christian Year, we followers of Jesus remember places in Palestine where important events took place in His life and ministry. We claim those places as ours, because what happened there is what launched and now enables our own spiritual journey. The journey begins in Bethlehem. Without Bethlehem, our Lord's birth has no reality. Without Nazareth, we cannot place His nurturing and His preparation for His life mission to save us. Without Capernaum, we would not understand how shocking it was that He used as His home base the very place which Isaiah 9:1-2 called the darkest, the forgotten, the marginalized place (Zebulun and Naphtali). Without a second-story guest room in Jerusalem, we would not be able to see ourselves in the family where we belong, sitting with Him around His table. Without a garden outside Jerusalem called Gethsemane, we would not know He prayed His heart out before He gave Himself over to a horrible, yet saving death. Without a small hill called Golgotha, we would not know we are healed, because He was broken. Without a stone tomb outside Jerusalem, we would not know the miracle that opened the way to eternity.

We don't worship these sites, but we sure do love them. They give concreteness to the story of Jesus. They place us in His story, in His world, in His Kingdom—where we find our true selves, or rather, our true souls.

The story we're considering today is the story of a journey to a particular place. Luke tells us that the Roman emperor demanded a census of his great empire. He also tells us that since Joseph is a descendant of David, he and Mary have to travel to Bethlehem, David's city. It's a three-day trip, and because Mary is well advanced in her pregnancy, we assume she rides a donkey—a humble beast that is extremely reliable in that rough terrain. They arrive safely, but the town is packed. Imagine all the descendants of David flocking there for the census! Sorry, no rooms available. Finally, some innkeeper takes a little pity on their plight. He can't kick another family out of a room they've paid for, but he does own a stable. At least they'll have a roof over them.

In the overall scheme of things, this journey of two people to a fairly obscure place in an outer region of the great Roman Empire seems, well, inconsequential. Luke and John see it differently. What is happening on that journey is taking place in a woman's womb, and then in a tiny town and in a humble stable being prepared for the woman's baby. And all four Gospel witnesses say this birth in an out-of-the-way place, inside a crude stable with unsanitary hay, scruffy creatures great and small, and exposure to outside threats, will change the world.

The Empire is saturated with magnificent cities and impressive tabernacles of worship. God, however, chooses one of the most obscure locations possible for Christ's birthing. He chooses one of the least politically significant parts of the Empire. His birth room is a stable. His bed, to quote Dix's carol, is "a manger rude and bare." He much prefers the humble places—and, in fact, the everyday places of our own lives are perfect for a visit from Jesus.

The story of Jesus reveals that the more impressive places of the world give Him and His disciples the most resistance. The combined religious and government institutions of Jerusalem crucify Jesus and stone His disciples. The government in Rome crucifies and slaughters Christians as convenient scapegoats and for public entertainment. Strong Christian faith grows best in the smaller places and among the poor and powerless of the big cities. Big government, big cities and big religion honor power—their own. True followers of Jesus honor the God who incarnates Himself in poverty, humility and simplicity. And the places they most honor are not the places where Christianity becomes politically and institutionally powerful. They are places like a stable in Bethlehem, a carpenter's shop and a very small synagogue in Nazareth, some small towns and a mountaintop somewhere in

Galilee, the home of a disreputable tax collector, a small garden, a hill, a tomb outside Jerusalem and a lakeside fishing spot. These are worth remembering, because they are places outside the halls of worldly power, where miracles take place and people are forever changed by a very different kind of power.

We live in a world of important small places, but a screen-centered society wants us to move on. It is a society that pressures us to abandon the concrete specifics of living and float around from one tentative place to another and from one internet "encounter" to another. The difference between our world and that of Jesus is not simply a difference of technology and mobility. It is a difference in how we locate ourselves in the world in which we live. We may all too rarely stop in one place and patiently listen to God, or ourselves, or another person. We may all too rarely realize we're in a place that God is invading with a burning bush or a tongue of fire. We may be so distracted in the very place God has placed us that we simply miss Him altogether. Maybe we're waiting for the perfect place or the spectacular setting—forgetting about the unspectacular places where Jesus set about changing the world. Maybe we need simply to be where we are, and in that real place, hear His voice, look Him in the face, and start obeying.

Our spiritual journeys must be grounded in the everyday world, as was Jesus' own life. We must look around us and see something as if for the first time, hear something we've never heard that way, talk with someone as we've never talked with them before, open our hearts in a way that surprises us, say something that penetrates a barrier. We could start right now. God would be with us.

Prayer

Dear Lord, thank You for loving me in the place I am. Please give me the patience to pause in the places I find myself today, then to listen to Your voice, see who or what You want me to see, be who You want me to be, and love who or what You want me to love. Free me from the drivenness that prevents me from placing myself where You have placed me. Please come to me this ordinary day in an extraordinary way. I ask in the name of Jesus, my down-to-earth, extraordinary Lord. Amen.

"Nearby shepherds were living in the fields, guarding their sheep by night... The angel said, 'Don't be afraid! Look! I bring good news to you—wonderful joyous news for all people'" (Luke 2:8, 10).

DECEMBER 24 (CHRISTMAS EVE)
Unto Whom?
Scripture—Luke 2:8-20

On this day, we celebrate the Miracle we've been waiting for. We call it "the Miracle," because for the first and only time in human history, God and man became one. We also call it the Miracle, because all the miracles that ensued over the course of Jesus' life were made possible by this one miraculous Birth. The whole story of Jesus is the continuation of this Miracle we call Incarnation, the enfleshment of God—Immanuel, God with us. Jesus, Son of God and Man.

We should also say that this Miracle of miracles came in quite a peculiar way. As we saw in yesterday's meditation, the very location of Jesus' birth does not suggest suitability for an important event in history. We'd expect the Jewish Messiah would be born in Jerusalem, the center of Jewish faith and worship. Instead, Luke's gospel spotlight travels to little Bethlehem, and not to its better homes and inns, but to a stable.

As if all this wasn't odd enough, things get downright weird as Luke leads us from the humble birthing stable out to even more obscure terrain, where the only people who are tough and desperate enough to hang out are crude herdsmen—in particular, shepherds. We're talking the lowest rung on the social and economic ladder—the humblest of the poor. We're talking coarse, dirty and smelling of sheep. People unaccustomed to civilized worship and holy living. The last group you'd want at your nice family gatherings.

The angel of the Lord shines the spotlight on *them*! In order to find worshipers and witnesses of this never-before-seen-God-in-the-human-flesh-of-a-baby, the angel goes out looking—and finds shepherds. He scrapes the bottom of the barrel of human society—people who know practically nothing about Scripture and rarely go to worship, if at all.

As hardened as these outdoor herdsmen are, watch their reaction when the angel shows up and showers them with glowing glory. They are scared stiff. Their rugged fortitude has not prepared them for this! They are probably temporarily blinded by the glory. Then the angel says what angels love to say: "Don't be afraid." And then he delivers the message: "I've got good news—wonderful, joyous news for everyone [in other words, even and especially you shepherds]! Your Savior is born this very night . . . Christ the Lord! Go and see. It's not very far from here. Look for a stable with some light, and see if you can find a newborn baby, wrapped snugly and lying in a manger with Mom and Dad nearby."

No sooner has the message been delivered than a choir of heavenly forces bursts on the scene and fills the sky with an anthem: "Glory to God in Heaven, and on Earth peace among those whom He favors." As quickly as the choir has appeared, they disappear, leaving the shepherds to decide whether or not to go look for a baby Messiah. They don't hesitate. "Let's go right now," they say to each other. "Let's see. Let's confirm." They leave immediately, and they find Mary and Joseph—and a small, fragile newborn Messiah, divinity in swaddling clothes.

Luke doesn't say of them, as Matthew says of the three Magi, that they kneel and worship Jesus. The Magi are astrologers and contemplatives. The shepherds are men of action, so they act. Luke says that they start reporting what they've seen and what they've been told this birth means. They must be telling the story in a convincing way, because everyone who hears it is amazed. The last we hear of these shepherds is that they return home "glorifying and praising God."

Have you ever wondered what happened to them? They may have not lived long enough to see and hear Jesus when He began His saving mission thirty years later. Most shepherds of that day probably did not have a long life span. It was a very hard life in the wild. The Gospels say no more about them. Perhaps they lived the rest of their earthly lives by the promise revealed in the illumined straw that night. Perhaps they were stunned into the revelation that they, the lowliest, were the first to hear the angels—first to obey, first to see, first to proclaim. The first witnesses—witnesses who believed, because they actually saw the Child.

When Jesus did begin His mission about thirty years later, He talked about a shepherd. He called Him "the good shepherd," and He said He was that shepherd—the shepherd who cares for His sheep and would even give His life for them. As a boy, Jesus had plenty of opportunities to observe shepherds, and He saw in the best of them the qualities that would shape His heart and His ministry. The Church later took the name of shepherd (pastor) to describe its spiritual leaders. Truth be told, the name could be applied to the calling of every follower of Jesus. We all have someone to shepherd, love, care for, give our lives to. Maybe those common shepherds who came from the hillside that night almost two thousand years ago received such love, such goodness and such grace that they became good shepherds for the Shepherd and Guardian of their souls.

Today, we celebrate the coming of our Savior in human

flesh—Jesus, who became our Good Shepherd and privileged a group of ordinary shepherds to have first sight and be first witnesses. This Birth humbles us, strips away our arrogance and pride, because we ourselves are the unworthy ones on that hillside, brought to the manger as we are, called to be shepherds for the Good Shepherd.

This Christmas Eve night, look up to the sky. Let yourself see angels singing. They're singing to you. If you feel as lowly as those first shepherds did, know that the good news comes first to you. If you feel all too good about your position and accomplishments, know that this night tells you who you really are: no better than those who think they're the least, but privileged to be one of them.

Prayer

Dear Jesus, who came in humility and was revealed to lowly shepherds, teach me to see myself among the least, so that I can know myself for whom I really am—one of Your beloveds, made precious not by anything I have done but by the value You give me through the life You lived and the death You suffered for us all.

This Christmas Eve, I come again to the stable of Your birth, awed by the Miracle and overwhelmed by Your presence right here with us. Teach me to be like those first shepherds, a living witness that You have indeed come into the world. May my actions show the difference Your presence can make in one person's life. I pray this through You, my Lord, my Shepherd. Amen.

"... the people who lived in the dark have seen a great light, and a light has come upon those who lived in the region and in the shadow of death." (Matthew 4:16)

STAGE TWO

LIVING CHRISTMAS

Thirteen Beginning Days

A Prayer for the Christmas Season
(This prayer anticipates the journey of these thirteen days.)
Lord, during the Advent season, I've been praying and preparing myself
for You to come this Christmas season in a fresh, new, even revolutionary way,
not in the outworn ways of my conformity and compromises.
As I look forward to these days, I ask that You will:
Transform me through the clean brightness of Your appearing.
Enrich my heart and life to include and care for others.
Give me the vision to see You calling out to me in my neighbor
and the courage to respond with Jesus' neighbor love.
Give me Your vision for the world and Your compassion for
every race and ethnicity.
Teach me the grace and goodness of living inclusively and the freedom of
letting the unique light that I am through Christ shine brightly.
Give me gratitude for Your countless gifts of which I am so undeserving.
Captivate my consciousness by the promises sung by angels at Jesus' birth.
Overcome my fear with the contentment of Your strong love.
Help me to blend the sweet with the bitter in my life, just as Jesus showed me.
Give me Jesus' humility and lack of self-serving pretense.
Fill my life with deep joy, even when there is no obvious reason for it.
And help me to keep my eye on that Bethlehem star so that, like those Magi,
I will find You in Your vulnerable divinity and be reminded that You have
also called me to lay down my life and, in doing so, find life.
I pray this through the One whose birth brought purpose
and hope to the world.
Amen.

DECEMBER 25 (CHRISTMAS DAY)
The Dawn: Living in the Brightness
Scripture—Luke 1:78b-79; Matthew 4:12-17

I love the dawn. I love the way it begins as a slight glimmer on the horizon and then gradually expands to fill the skies with the gift of a new day. I love it when it glows red, giving us breathtaking beauty at the start. I love it when it sparkles in crystal clarity, seeming to promise a kind of purity. I don't love sunrise as much when the emerging light is diminished by cloud cover, as if to rob us of the beauty and the clarity or perhaps depress us a bit. Even then, however, we know the sun is there, and plenty of light gets through. We can't hold back the dawn.

The coming of the Son of God into the world in Jesus of Nazareth was like the dawning of a new day. It *was* a new day! Everything changed. John's Gospel announces that on this morning we celebrate today, Jesus, the embodied Son of God, shined inextinguishably in this dark world—shined on all people (John 1:5-9). In Luke's Gospel, Zechariah, just months before Jesus' birth, looked to the near future and announced that " … the dawn from heaven will break upon us,/ to give light to those who are sitting in darkness/ and in the shadow of death, to guide us in the path of peace." And in Matthew's Gospel, Jesus, who had confined His mission to Judea of the Jews, turned His attention to Galilee of the Gentiles. The writer describes this crucial move in the words of Isaiah's prophecy: "the people who lived in the dark have seen a great light,/ and a light has come upon those who live in the region and in the shadow of death." And for nine chapters in Luke's Gospel, Jesus returned to Jerusalem for crucifixion through Samaria, a locale despised as spiritually contaminated by citizens with mixed Jewish and Gentile ancestry. The Light is for everyone.

The Light can neither be extinguished, nor confined. Admittedly, in some times and places, it has seemed a small, fragile light, but the glow will never be extinguished. The dawn of God's Kingdom of life and love has begun with the birth of Him who is the very Light of the World (John 8:12)—Him who brings His light wherever He is, overcoming the darknesses of our world (Revelation 16:33).

The question for us is this: *How do we live in the brightness?* Christmas is the Christian's spiritual dawn. It calls us to a life flooded with true light. A man named Paul was on his way to Damascus to persecute members of this new Christian movement when he was overwhelmed with "a light from heaven." The force of it knocked him to the ground, and the Light of the World, now resurrected, asked him why he was trying to extinguish the Light. Blinded and humbled by the brightness, he regained his sight in a few days and began a radical change (Acts 9:3-6). He started to live in the Light. The Light exposed his arrogance and the fear behind his hatred. The exposure was painful, but the Light was compassionate—drawing him to forgiveness. He spent the rest of his life shining the Light, at great personal cost and suffering, across a darkened Mediterranean world.

How can we, like Paul, live in the brightness that Christ brought into the world on the day we now commemorate? We can begin by observing this day for what it really is: a celebration of the Dawn. Christmas Day is many different things to many different people. For some, it is little more than a day of eagerly opening gifts from friends and relatives and enjoying a sumptuous feast. Indeed, gift-giving can be a wonderful reminder of our gift-giving God. He teaches us to open our gifts celebrating the love behind them, not the unimportant material value. We celebrate the Dawn when we receive love that can't be measured. We also celebrate the Dawn when we gather around the family table for Christmas dinner, not only to enjoy God's gift of delicious food lovingly prepared, but also to allow the brightness to open our hearts to a larger, more inclusive family—even, perhaps, to invite a guest we otherwise would not think to include in our small circle. We celebrate the Dawn when we see beyond our narrow lighting.

We live in the brightness when we allow ourselves to see differently. What we see is influenced by how we see. The lens through which we see shapes our perceptions. People sometimes see falsely as they may predispose themselves to see. The Light that dawned on the first Christmas morning reveals truth—truth that exposes our sin and self-seeking, truth that calls us to confess our sins and humble ourselves in the embrace of God's love. Those who live in the brightness don't fear what the Light will expose. Christ is the lens of their honesty and the forgiver of their failures. They allow themselves to see what Christ sees, and under this exposing Light, they see more of who they can be in Christ.

We live in the brightness when our living authenticates the Light. "Live your life as children of light," said Paul (Ephesians 5:8b). "Get rid of the actions that belong to the darkness and put on the weapons of light" (Romans 13:12b). John promised that " … if we live in the light in the same way as He [God] is in the light, we have fellowship with each other, and the blood of Jesus, His Son, cleanses us from every sin" (I John 1:7). The most amazing thing of all is that we are actually called to *be* light. "You are the light of the world," says Jesus invitingly to His would-be disciples (Matthew 5:14a).

Finally, we live in the brightness by reflecting it. It is well known and documented that holidays are often stressful times within families. Closer company can create tension. High holiday expectations not sufficiently realized can cause frustration. The buildup before

Christmas can so exhaust us as to make us vulnerable to outbursts of temper. Confessions and apologies are certainly in order for the holiday season if needed. Living in the brightness of the Dawn is a matter of reflecting it. We followers of Jesus are not called simply to absorb the Light. We are called to burn with the brightness of His love, to see Him in one another, to allow Him to live His life in us. To reflect Him.

Christmas Day is a good day to begin living in the brightness, or to nurture it even further. Christ the Light is here among us!

Prayer

Dear Lord, especially on this Christmas Day, this day of Light—I want to shine with Your brightness. I want to do so every day of my life, even on those days that are not working out so well for me. Today, I want to hold the Christ Child in my arms and take in the light of His love, receive the gift of His grace and be empowered by His Spirit.

I pray for my family and friends whose fellowship I will enjoy during the days of Christmas. May I gratefully receive the blessing of their lives and seek to bless theirs. I pray also for others whom I know but am not close to. Help me to know and appreciate them more. Help me to see Christ in them and in whatever way I humbly can, be Christ to them. And I especially pray for those outside my orbit, especially those who suffer and those who know You not. Help me to see that they are not outside Your orbit or Your love, and motivate me to support those who have given their lives to reaching them. I pray this in the name of our Light-giving, world-embracing Lord Jesus. Amen.

DECEMBER 26

AT HOME: LIVING WITH A LARGER FAMILY

Scripture—Matthew 2:16-23; Luke 2:41-52

Families are important during these days of Christmas. Jesus Himself was part of a family. He was not some extraterrestrial being who was beamed down directly from the beyond, unassisted by human hands. He came the human way, born into a family. When the shepherds and later the Magi came to visit Him, they found a *family*, as did anyone who visited during those days. Too many Nativities strike me as posed, as if the scene was locked in time and space, and the Holy Child was an object that couldn't actually be touched. Rembrandt's *The Adoration of the Shepherds* gives a very different picture: everyone crowded around the manger, leaving almost no space between them, moving, talking, wondering—like one big, ever-expanding holy family. And it includes shepherds!

Early in our marriage, Keitha and I visited my relatives in England during the Christmas season. I had never met these relatives. They were extremely gracious to invite us to stay in their homes. I was curious about my English ancestry and was grateful to meet so many of my relations "across the pond." I was also interested in some of the English customs. One of them, Boxing Day, is observed December 26th, the day after Christmas Day. I had never heard of it. It is not a day to fight (box); it is a day to give boxes—that is, Christmas gifts. It is said to have originated as a way for families with servants to give presents (in boxes) to those servants and their families, along with the day off for the families to have their own family Christmas together. Over time, the practice expanded, and many citizens became accustomed to giving gifts to people who provided them services but weren't actual employees of those citizens (for example: postal workers, sanitary workers, etc.). This is what many of us do in the USA.

If there is something helpful to take from what is behind the Boxing Day tradition, it is the sense of expanding the family dimensions of Christmas. Christmas Day can be a very cozy family tradition in which we shut ourselves off from the rest of the world to enjoy the comfort of our family. There is nothing innately wrong with this. Family time is important to the season. Our Lord, however, wants us to be a part of a bigger family than our cozy few. Jesus' birthing stable was overrun with people from near and far. Do you actually think that the people who were "amazed" by what the shepherds gossiped about didn't rush off to see? Perhaps you could ask yourself: *How expansive is my family? Do my family members draw strength from each other to love others, include others, live for others? Or, is my family too heavily walled, inwardly turned, self-absorbed?*

We were in Kingston, Jamaica, visiting my parents one Christmas season. On Christmas Day morning before sunrise, we heard the soft, sonorous sound of a Jamaican male choir singing "Go Tell It on the Mountain" as they slowly danced single file through the neighborhood. They felt like family members awakening us, voices calling us to a larger Christmas praise and worship. After breakfast, we put on our Salvation Army uniforms and joined other Salvationists at the large city hospital, spending the rest of the morning singing carols and praying with patients. I remember nothing else about that Christmas Day, save, of course, the delicious family dinner my mother prepared for us. The remembrance of an early morning choir and gracious hospital patients still lingers in my mind as part of a family Christmas. On that Christmas Day, there was very little that had the feel of just our little family and much that had the feel of an expanding family. The Light that has shined in the darkness has given us larger families and more friends to whom we have reached out. Without them, we live in a small, suffocating family enclosure.

Matthew brought Herod, the reigning eastern agent of the oppressive Roman government, into the Christmas story. Herod didn't mind breaking up a family. He heard rumors about a Jewish Messiah, and because of his obsession with power, he saw such a Messiah to be a threat to his part of the Empire. So, he tried to persuade the Magi to give him information of this person's whereabouts when they found Him, so he also could worship Him. The Magi were warned in a dream of Herod's real motivation, so they returned to their home in the east by a different route. Herod, determined to destroy the Child, ordered all male children in Bethlehem who were two and under to be slaughtered. When an angel warned them of this impending slaughter, Joseph and Mary fled with their Child to Egypt and stayed there until Herod's death. We don't know what happened to the family in Egypt during those years. They probably merged with other Jewish families and associated with some Gentile families. Returning to Nazareth in Galilee, they set up their home. Joseph set up his carpenter's shop, and Jesus undoubtedly trained as his apprentice. Other children came along; Jesus had brothers and sisters. He was part of a large family. And then at around thirty years of age, He set out on His own. Everything His family could do for Him, they had done; and everything He could do for them at that point, as son and brother, He had done. His greatest gift would come later, to be shared with the whole world, His larger family.

I wish we had more information about Jesus' family life during His first thirty years. We do know that at age twelve, Jesus had something of a clash with His parents. The family were on the way home. After a day's travel, His parents discovered that Jesus was not in the caravan. They panicked and returned to Jerusalem to find Him. They finally discovered Him in the temple, sitting with the elders, listening and asking questions, and amazing everyone with His understanding. Keep in mind that the age of twelve was when a child was considered an adult. Jesus was showing signs of independence. He had become more oriented toward doing His heavenly Father's business than the family business. He began the separation which every child of a healthy family must undergo. But He remained in Joseph's carpenter shop for seventeen more years, preparing His heart and mind to fulfill His calling. Indeed, He was a gift to His family, as they were to Him. And then the time came for Him to expand the family *He* was birthing by giving Himself to and for the whole world.

How can you and I help Jesus enlarge His family? Not so much by our teaching and preaching as by our *living*. Is there a way we can celebrate our participation in Jesus' larger family today, as well as during this twelve-day Christmas season? And could we continue over our lives to nurture the reach of our family with the inclusive love of Jesus?

Prayer

Dear Lord, we thank You for our families. Some of us have had loving families who nurtured and taught us well. Others of us were not raised in such families; we're grateful we found another family or other families who became our better families. My prayer this day is for You to enlarge me and the family I claim. Make me an inclusive influence toward those with whom I live and serve, and empower me to be a champion for the open-armed Christ whose Kingdom is love. I ask this in His name. Amen.

DECEMBER 27

IN THE NEIGHBORHOOD: LIVING NEXT DOOR

Scripture—John 1:14a; Romans 13:8-10

Think about nearness. Think about God. Then put the two together. "The Lord is near," says the apostle Paul (Philippians 4:5b). "The Word became flesh and made His home among us" (John 1:14a)—literally, "pitched His tent among us." In other words: Christ is present with our next door neighbors and with all our neighbors. As followers of Jesus, our relationships with our neighbors cannot be neutral. Our calling is not simply to behave ourselves around them, be respectful and be nice. Our essential calling is to find Christ around or in them, and as best as we can, be Christ to them.

Let's remember that at Christmastide, we celebrate this cohabiting God of ours. We sing "O Come, O Come, Emmanuel," which is a boldfaced statement that "God is near." If you want to see the nearness of God, look at Jesus, God in flesh and blood—close enough to give us the comfort and assurance we need at times, and close enough to cause the discomfort and disturbance we need at times. During times of prayerful solitude with God, His nearness may give us the peace our hearts long for, or it may prod us to be honest and confess our failures and ask for His enabling grace. During times when we are with our neighbors, we may sense we are working alongside our Lord, or we may be disturbed in spirit, because we sense He is revealing to us that we are not being Christlike and not being the love-driven neighbors He wants us to be.

A previous meditation spoke of our increasingly privatized world, now further enabled by the internet. In this self-absorbed world, we are trained to be sensitive to someone's needs only when we can play upon those needs for our own advantage. Reuel Howe once said: "God made people to be loved and things to be used, but we turn it around; we all too often love things and use people." If we do not hear God weeping over this perversion of our humanity, we aren't listening.

For a Christian to be aware is for her to *see* Christ in the person or the situation in which she finds herself. For a Christian to be a Christian (a true disciple of Jesus) is for her to *be* Christ to the person or in the situation. We may call ourselves Christians, but if we see our Christian faith as only a private affair between us and God, we are sadly and tragically misguided. To ignore our neighbors or our neighborhoods is to ignore Jesus Himself and to nullify most of His teachings. It is, in fact, to reject what He commands us to do, and therefore to reject Him as our Lord. As we've already seen, loving our God is paired with loving our neighbors as much as we love ourselves (Mark 12:29-31). John hits the target with an even sharper arrow: We are liars when we say we love God while not loving a brother or sister (I John 4:20). And Jesus went even further, adding our enemies to the list of people we must love (Matthew 5:44)!

John Wesley, the Father of the modern-day Holiness movement, liked to emphasize that Christianity is a social religion. What he meant was that it has to do with every human relationship we have. The Christian faith by its very nature is lived out in all those relationships. Holiness is as social as it is personal. Without both, holiness is—well, not holiness. Jesus came into the neighborhood so that He could enter our lives, and He entered our lives so that He could lead us *back* into our neighborhoods to cohabit with Him. Our neighborhoods are where He calls us out to be with Him.

You can totally ignore a neighbor, even one next door. It happens all the time. People living alone have died in their homes and not been discovered until weeks later. For those who ignored them, they hardly existed. People can even live in the same house and barely know each other. You can ignore a very close neighbor. What good is it that God has come to dwell in our neighborhoods to reach every neighbor if we don't hear Him calling us to embody His caring presence with our own neighbors? How can we be Jesus' imitating disciples if we do not follow Him by reaching out to those around us?

One of the most interesting Nativity paintings I've seen is in the National Gallery of Art in Washington, D.C. It's Savoldo's *The Adoration of the Shepherds*. What is striking is that the faces of everyone in the scene are lit up brightly. There is no discernible source of the light, until you realize that it emanates from the face of the Christ Child.

If only we could see that brightness of Christ shining on the faces of our neighbors. If only we could grasp how important Jesus has made us all by coming to dwell with us. If only, by loving our neighbors, we could help them see and experience the light of God's love in their own lives. If only we could believe and live what the apostle Paul says: "You must love your neighbor as yourself" (Romans 13:9c). In fact, says Paul, the only debt we should owe anyone is "the obligation to love each other" (v. 8a). Loving our neighbors is never a credit, always a debit.

God took a huge risk when He laid aside the armor of divinity and became one of us. He set Himself up for ridicule, hurt, disappointment and execution. "God with us" came with an exorbitant price tag. Love, however, never fails (I Corinthians 13:8a), never draws back. Whenever we see a neighbor as God does, we also see the living, vulnerable Christ inviting us to be a Christlike neighbor.

Neighborhoods used to be intimate communities where people knew each other, helped each other, often made sacrifices for each other. Some still are, but there seems to be fewer of them. Keitha and I have as friends a couple who moved into a neighborhood of townhomes a few years ago. The community is multiethnic, multiracial and interfaith. Our friends didn't just settle in. They reached out. They built relationships. The wife offered to clean homes—one way you really get to know people! They founded a big community event during the Christmas season. Both their faith and their compassion are well known in that now more close-knit community.

Perhaps now, more than ever, we need Christian disciples who do more than locate in the neighborhoods where they live. Christ invites us to be concerned parts of our communities, sources of genuine neighborliness, people of hospitality and compassion, lovers of Jesus, and people who love like Jesus.

What do you say, neighbor? More importantly, what is God saying?

Prayer

Dear neighboring God, give me the courage to stick my neck out to reach out to a neighbor I'm not so inclined to contact. Help me to see him or her as Christ does, with unbiased eyes and a compassionate heart. Give me a good opportunity, as unsure as I may be about it, and the introductory words, as imperfectly as I may say them, to cross the bridge to a relationship that You will make possible. I trust You to help me take it from there and follow wherever You lead. I ask this in the name of Jesus, who never knew a stranger. Amen.

DECEMBER 28

IN THE WORLD: LIVING EVERYWHERE

Scripture—John 3:16-17; Matthew 28:16-20; Luke 2:32a

When Jesus tells us to "love our neighbors as we love ourselves," we may not fully understand the extent of it. We may wonder how near a person needs to be in order to be our neighbor. A lawyer wanted Jesus to give a definition, a better measure so that he could be clear about the extent of his neighborly obligation. Jesus answered, of course, with a story. You know it well: a man went down from Jerusalem to Jericho. He was attacked by thieves, stripped naked, beaten and left for dead. A priest passed by without helping, then a Levite, and finally the third passerby—a despised-by-the-Judean-Jews Samaritan—stopped. He stopped because he was overcome with compassion. Without pausing to consider the cultural and religious differences separating him from the wounded man, he tended to the man's wounds, slaked his thirst, took him to an inn, paid for further housing and care, and guaranteed he would make good on any further costs to the innkeeper when he passed by on the way home.

Who is neighbor to this man? The lawyer gave the right answer: the one who showed mercy (Luke 10:25-37). What is not to be missed in this story is that Jesus did not so much describe who a neighbor is as what it looks like to *be* a neighbor to anyone, not so much what a neighborhood looked like as what neighbor-ness looked like. If we talk about people we live near (in our neighborhood), or people with whom we are acquainted, we're not getting the whole picture. A neighbor is anyone in need of whom we become aware.

This makes it awfully difficult to set any kind of geographical limits on who the neighbor is whom Jesus calls us to love. The wounded man by the side of the road is, by the customs of that day, outside the Samaritan's orbit of life and influence, and the Samaritan was under no civilized obligation to expose himself to danger by getting involved. This provocative, barrier-breaking teaching of Jesus helps us understand why Simeon, lifting the infant Jesus in his arms in the temple, describes Him as "a light for revelation to the Gentiles." The Gentiles were those outside the orbit of a narrow religious nationalism. Jesus spoke of Himself as a shepherd of "one flock," referring to Jews who received Him as Messiah. He then went on to speak of having "*other* sheep that don't belong to this sheep pen," undoubtedly meaning Gentiles (everyone else). Together they will be "one flock, with one shepherd" (John 11:11-16). It sounds suspiciously like a flock with no borders.

Some Jews in Palestine did not receive this message gladly. They were nationalists who wanted to be rid of their pagan Roman oppressors and enjoy an exclusively Jewish kingdom, and they expected their promised Messiah to set it up. This is quite understandable given the oppression under which they had been suffering for a long time. Some Jews did become disciples of Jesus and over time had to come to terms with the Gospel's inclusiveness, as did even the twelve disciples (Peter especially). Ironically, over the centuries, the Jews themselves became a scattered people without a nation. Within a relatively short period of time, they were stereotyped as the enemies of Christ, persecuted, slaughtered, exiled—much to the shame of we who call ourselves followers of Jesus, who was Himself a Jew. Fast-forward to our 21st century, and we see the rising tide of nationalism in the USA giving encouragement to extremist white nationalists who perpetrate violence against those who don't look like them or worship as they do. The very week I write this meditation, the eleven victims of the Tree of Life Synagogue shootings in Pittsburgh are being laid to rest. The alleged perpetrator is a white nationalist and anti-Semite. God help us!

From the very beginning of its existence, the Christian Church has struggled with Jesus' challenge of an across-the-border, expansive neighbor-ness. We are more comfortable associating with people like us. Associating with people "not like us" or "not from around here" is far more difficult and threatening. This is why some church growth groups have recommended growing our churches by reaching out to homogeneous (just-like-us) groups. Call it growth by choosing the more comfortable path of least resistance. Jesus, however, knew His Old Testament. He remembered that God obligated His people to accept and care for the aliens or strangers in their midst, remembering that they themselves were once strangers. (See, for example, Exodus 23:9 and Deuteronomy 10:18.) And He obviously knew that the only way His Gospel would take root across our planet—the whole world God so loves—was for Christians like us to reach out to people not like us. Why else would the resurrected Jesus command His small band of Jewish disciples to get over their nationalist prejudices, and go and make disciples of *all ethnicities* (Matthew 28:19a)?

It began with Christians who were willing to be the kind of neighbors who take the risk of being Christ's hands of compassion for people not like them—people who live in a different world or have different outlooks. Come to think of it, Jesus Himself was an alien in the culture of His day. He was so out of sync with it that one Gospel writer says, "The light [Jesus] came to His own people, and His own people didn't welcome Him" (John 1:11). In the end, He was abandoned, turned against. His attitude was so radically expansive and compassionate that when most people saw it, they were drawn to retreat into spiritual complacency and self-protection. And then it got Him killed. But there is something about how, why and for whom He died that began to draw people back—people who were willing to be aliens and exiles in the world (I Peter 2:11a), like Jesus. Those who have this creative distance from the current world order are in a position to help bring the kind of transformation that is Jesus' true mission.

It begins with compassion toward those who are not like us—people whose otherness we do not allow to threaten us, engender hatred in us and distance us. Who in the world is that "other" for you? What do you hear your Lord saying about him or her? And what will you do to show that "other" the love that Jesus showed his neighbors?

Prayer
Dear Christ, our God Incarnate, help us today to see
Your face in those not like us: these, too, You long to free.
We hear the call to love You by bringing them close by.
In touching them we also touch the Christ who in them lies.
Amen.

DECEMBER 29

For Everyone: Living Inclusively

Scripture—Luke 1:46-55; Titus 2:11

As Christmas people, we can no longer live in denial of certain realities. One reality is what the verse above from Titus says in one large inclusive sweep: "The grace of God has appeared, *bringing salvation to all people*" (italics added). Everyone was included, no one excluded from the scope of this story that began in a small Jewish town during the first Christmas. This Christ Child was the divine Seed of saving grace, planted in Mary, then Palestine, and from there sown around the world. To paraphrase the words of John's Gospel, Christ brought inextinguishable light and life for the entire human race (John 1:3c-5). Christians are people who live in the reality of this all-inclusive saving grace of God in Christ.

Another reality is that the everywhere-ness of God affects every moment and every place in our day. Centuries ago, Meister Eckhart said it this way:

> A man may go into the field and say his prayers and be aware of God; or he may be in church and be aware of God. But if he is more aware of God because he is in a quiet place, that is his own deficiency and not due to God, Who alike is present in all things and all places, and is willing to give Himself everywhere, so far as lies in Him. He knows God rightly who knows Him everywhere. (*The Sermons*)

To know God in our quiet, undisturbed times, to know Him when we are surrounded by a community of fellow Christians, and to know

Him in the assuring majesty and adoration of worship is one thing. To know God in a pagan world that isn't ready-made for Christian solitude, God talk, the support of fellow disciples, or anything resembling Christian worship is the gift of the God who in Christ is now everywhere. "My name is joined to Thine by *every human tie*," writes Albert Orsborn in one of his songs (*SASB* 79, v. 2., italics added). Wherever we are, whoever we're with—Christ is present. Do we hear or see Him? Do we allow ourselves to be present with Him in that moment?

Here, then, is another reality of this inclusive living: it is more than a state of mind; it is a call to action. It is crossing a border, venturing into the unknown, breaking the rules of confining social interaction. It is looking into the heart of a stranger and inviting him to be our guest. It is personalizing an otherwise perfunctory relationship. It is action at a deeper level propelled by a search for Christ where and in whom He is strangely and surprisingly present. Christmas people know that what got started in Bethlehem streams everywhere on our planet, waiting for disciples to look for it and act on it. We live every day in the question: *Where is Christ in this particular place?* We encounter a despised person and reach out to her, because she is the marginalized Christ at that moment. We reach out to an abusive person, because Christ alone, who stands beside all the abused and was Himself abused, is the one who can free the abuser from the damaged heart that drives him to hurt others. The Christ we know to be present everywhere calls us to act as if He is.

Another reality that proclaims and challenges our inclusiveness is expressed in the lines of a hymn: "Christ for the world, we sing; the world to Christ we bring" (*SASB*, 917). The hymn was written at a time when the Church (including The Salvation Army) saw bringing the Gospel to other races and ethnicities primarily as something

Western Christians did overseas or on a different continent. For the most part, in our country, minority races worshiped in congregations comprised of their own race. In our 21st-century world, other races and ethnicities have immigrated to Western countries, and many of our church congregations are beginning to look more racially diverse, while others seem set on "racially pure" gatherings of the faithful. "Christ for the world" may be something we believe and sing, but when the world comes to our congregation, the words become an up-front-and-personal challenge. Did God ever intend for Sunday morning worship to be the most segregated gathering in our nation? When the Kingdom of God comes in its fullness, all races from north and south, east and west will come together and sit down around the same table of fellowship (Luke 13:29). Are we to have no foretaste of it till that time comes? If Christ came to bring us together (Ephesians 1:9-10; Colossians 3:9b-11), a unity enriched by its diversity, should we not bring this future into the present, for our own good and the good of the world?

I hasten to add that though opening our congregations to racial inclusion is absolutely the right thing to do, inviting the entire congregation to be a part of conversations about this decision is an act of wisdom on our part and a sign of respect for each member. Furthermore, underlying the plan must be a strategy to succeed. Good intentions without practices to create a welcoming and inclusive family environment, for example, will likely end in failure.

A final reality that challenges our inclusiveness is to hear Mary's poetic *Magnificat* for what it is: *the lifting of the poor and lowly and the humbling of the rich and mighty.* It all begins when lowly Mary is highly favored as the birth mother of the long-awaited Messianic King. She can hardly believe that God "has looked with favor on

[her] low estate" in life. She, the humblest, is now the "highly favored." The merciful God is flexing His arm to lift her up. But it is not just her He is lifting up. He is lifting up the ranks of the lowly and filling the hungry with good things. At the same time, He is scattering the arrogant people who hold the power, pulling them down from their thrones, and sending the rich away empty-handed.

So is this some kind of radical political agenda? The life of Jesus gives us no indication that He is interested in such. Politics has to do with governance; Jesus is interested in godliness. The godly live by the power of divine love, not by the love of worldly power. With no more than the weapons of spiritual warfare, the godly stand up to the powermongers of this world on behalf of the victims of those who abuse power. They stand with the lowly, because they are the ones God lifts up to honor, and the powerful are those He brings down to humility, sooner or later. From a lowly stable to an outcast cross, the life of Jesus is an invitation to the banquet shared by all, the first being last, the last first—all brothers and sisters. Let we who follow Jesus model that courageous inclusiveness today.

Prayer
Dear Lifter of the lowly and Humbler of the mighty, please help me to align myself with Your agenda by opening my heart, my life and my church to the excluded and the marginalized. Help me to move beyond my own cultural biases and sinful prejudices to appreciate Your generous gifts of diversity and differences. Keep me from seeking the comfortableness of sameness and fearing the threat of change. Give me the courage to challenge embedded status quos and oppressive powers. I ask this in the name of He who faced up to the oppressors and paid the price with His life. Amen.

DECEMBER 30
THE BEAUTIFUL LIFE: LIVING HOLY
Scripture—I Corinthians 13

Let's begin this meditation by honoring good deeds. God loves for us to help others, to make this world a better place to live, to use the resources we have for the benefit of those who have little. In fact, Jesus is described as one who "went about doing good" (Acts 10:38). As we are called to imitate His life, doing good is a part of our calling as well (Ephesians 6:8).

There is more to be said, however, and it has to do with why people do good deeds. There are different reasons. They may have the gift of helping, so it comes naturally. They may feel sorry for someone. They may simply enjoy the reward that comes from helping. They may be trying to compensate for a poorly lived life. They may be trying to gain esteem in the community. For others, there may be a combination of some of these motives.

In this meditation, we are not considering the good things a person does—for whatever reason or desired outcome. We are considering who a person is rather than the good things she does. It is quite possible, after all is said and done, for someone to wear herself out doing good and still feel an emptiness, even a meaninglessness. The apostle Paul speaks of it in I Corinthians 13:3, where even an extreme excess of personal sacrifice comes to no benefit for the giver, because it doesn't flow from love. Paul describes this love, not in terms of actions we take on behalf of others, but first in terms of personal characteristics behind those actions (patience, kindness, being happy with the truth, putting up with all things, trusting in all things, hoping for all things, enduring all things) and then in terms of actions that a person chooses *not* to take (bragging, showing arrogance, getting irritable, keeping records of complaints, being happy about injustices) (vv. 4-7). There are no acts of love described here, only profiles of sanctified character. What is clear is that God looks not only on our good actions (what we do) but also on the heart (who we are).

Some Christians invest much in doing the right things and miss being the right people. They put usefulness ahead of holiness. Their love is practical and measurable, but it is not beautiful. Consider the woman who appeared suddenly at the Bethany dinner hosted by Simon and started anointing Jesus' head with costly perfume. The disciples were sure that the most practical use of the expensive ointment, worth almost a year's pay, would be to sell it and give the money to the poor, and they said so. Instead of indulging in this emotional display for attention, wouldn't it have been wiser for this woman to convert this ointment into money and have the gratification of feeding hundreds of hungry poor? The woman, probably unaware of the prudent option, continued anointing the head of Jesus. Jesus heard the criticism and put a curt stop to it. Receiving the woman's gift, He said, "She has done a beautiful thing to Me" (Matthew 26:10b; Mark 14:6b, NIV). The disciples saw the practical and measurable good that could be gained; Jesus saw the beautiful. He saw what was there in the woman's grateful, overflowing heart, and He said the world would forever remember the beauty of what she did (Mt. 26:13; Mk. 14:9).

The true beauty of a follower of Jesus is the beauty of love. The beauty of a church is the beauty of their all-encompassing love for God (Mark 12:30) reflected in their love for one another (John 13:34-35). The beauty of our mission is that we carry in our hearts the self-giving love God has for the world (John 3:16). The Salvation Army once described its mission in the world as "Compassion in Action." Compassion is not simply doing things for people in need; it is literally "*being with them* in their suffering." How do you measure that? You don't measure it; you honor the beauty of it and ask God for the grace of such a compassionate heart.

Each December, Jews observe the festival of Hanukkah in memory of the Maccabees' successful rebellion against their pagan oppressors and the rededication of the holy Temple (the Second Temple) following that victory. The temple was purified, and the wicks of the menorah burned for eight days, even though there was only enough sacred oil for one day's lighting. Hanukkah celebrates this miracle of sustained light—light that we do not produce by our own efforts. It is the act of God. It is pure and holy and beautiful in and of itself.

Holiness is not proven by the good things we do, though a holy person does good things. Holiness is proven by the beauty of a person's life. This is not the superficial beauty of being "good-looking" or having "a cultured way." It is a beauty fully accessible to those our surface world judges to be ugly and to those whose lack of education and social graces is undisguised. The beauty of holiness is not an appearance we can achieve or manufacture. It is the gift of God. It is Christ living in us, we allowing Him to humble our spirits, purify our motivations and to keep that change going. It is we, more and more, having a credible resemblance to Him—a genuine Christlikeness.

When Keitha and I served on the Salvation Army officer training college staff for the first time, I learned that for quite a few years, Albert Pepper had been the guest speaker for the annual holiness seminar. I had never heard Colonel Pepper preach, until he came for the seminar that year. His style was unassuming and very down to earth. His presentations were not scholarly. He did not engage in sophisticated articulations of the doctrine of holiness. He did not so much challenge our minds as penetrate our hearts. It did not take long for me to realize that Albert Pepper was not there to enlighten our intellectual grasp of the doctrine of sanctification. He was there to allow us to see the beauty of holiness convincingly embodied in a person. Holiness had become his nature, an effortless flow in and from him. He would say he was a recipient of the gift which he had done nothing to manufacture—like a Hanukkah candle with a God-given glow.

One of the prayer choruses we sing begins with the words "Let the beauty of Jesus be seen in me." The final lines say, "All my nature refine till the beauty of Jesus be seen in me." You and I are the Holy Spirit's refinements, and the model He uses is the heart of Jesus. What the Spirit seeks to gift us with is a genuine, deep, heart holiness more than practical applications of our religion. A pure heart is the goal and realization of our spiritual journey, and to the extent we resemble and reflect this holiness of Jesus, our lives glow with a true beauty.

Prayer

O Holy Child of Bethlehem, beautiful before You ever had a chance to do good, descend on me with the beauty of Your pure heart. Purify my own thoughts and motives, so that my life may reveal You, and any good I do may be seen as Your work in me. I pray this through You, the Light and Lover of the world. Amen.

"The Lord rules! Let the earth rejoice! Let all the islands celebrate! Clouds and thick darkness surround God. His throne is built on righteousness and justice" (Psalm 97:1-2).

DECEMBER 31 (NEW YEAR'S EVE)
Deep Gratitude: Living Thankfully

Scripture—Psalm 100; Ephesians 5:15-20; Hebrews 13:15

I remember the years when all corps used to have New Year's Eve Watch Night services. When Keitha and I were corps officers, we would plan two meetings with refreshments in between. The first meeting would include a report on the ways God had blessed us over the year and a time of testimony. It would sometimes include a more formal report on how successfully we had accomplished the goals we had set for the end of the year. The spirit of the meeting was one of gratitude. The spirit of the second meeting was one of expectation. We looked forward to the coming year. The goals were presented, the sermon encouraged a spirit of expectancy, and the meeting concluded with a time of prayer for the coming year. Soldiers (church members) who were able gathered around the Mercy Seat. (Today's meditation will focus on the theme of gratitude and living thankfully. The meditation for January 1st will focus on what it means to live in expectant hope as we begin the new year.)

The last day of the year is a day to say thank you to God. He has brought us through the year by His grace. He has blessed us in countless ways, most of which we are not even aware. His providence is often quiet, but never insignificant. We, all of us, are the recipients of grace upon grace.

Often, God sends us His grace through other people. I said thank you to my parents, but not enough. I try to say thank you to my wife Keitha, but I wish I did it as often as she deserved. A lot of relationships between spouses, families, friends and fellow workers go bad, because people take each other for granted and don't say thank you. Gratitude is not simply a polite and worthwhile social convention; it is at the heart of who we are as a family of a gracious and loving Father.

There are a lot of people who contributed to my life. I didn't know at the time to say thank you; and now they're gone. I wish I had said thank you to tall and slender Ms. Camp and short and stocky Ms. Alley, my second and third grade teachers at Adair Park Elementary School, who fired my passion for learning. I wish I had said thank you to my friend Bradley Wilson's mom, who tolerated my frequent visits to their fascinating, rambling old house on a corner, and introduced me to hominy and turnip greens and Southern hospitality. So many people and so many experiences fill our lives with gratitude.

Yes, I know there are other voices that question gratitude. There are some experiences and some people we're *not* thankful for. Maybe there has been a terrible accident with a tragic outcome. Grief over an untimely death. Abuse suffered at the hands of another. Dreams shattered for no good reason. A close relationship broken. It's all nice and dandy for someone to say to us, "Remember, all things work together for good . . ." We may want to respond, "I'm not ready to hear that, thank you." Sometimes, the only thing we have to be thankful for in such a situation is that we somehow got through it. Perhaps, we found a deeper grace in the midst of our hurting. Perhaps, we found our loving God right next to us, sharing or even bearing our pain—or He came in the flesh and blood of a caring person. Perhaps, down the road, we're ready to realize the experience made a better person of us—someone with more depth and greater compassion for the suffering around

December 31 (New Year's Eve)

us. Or, perhaps, we are still not over it.

Gratitude is not something we can self-generate. I cannot make myself grateful. Gratitude is God's gift to the humble of heart. By "the humble of heart," I don't mean those with low self-esteem. Demeaning ourselves is an insult to our Creator. The humble of heart are those who gratefully receive the gifts they don't deserve from a God they can't manipulate. There is no gratitude where the recipient thinks he's earned a blessing, nor where he's convinced he should have received more or better than he got, or should have received it sooner than he did. The grateful live in the joy of God's gifts, regardless of whether or not, by the standards of a materialistic, indulgent world, their storehouses are considered meager or their positions lowly.

In the Christian calendar, the year actually begins with Advent, which prepares us for the journey to Bethlehem to receive God's greatest gift to a fallen race. *This* is where our gratitude focuses—on the Christ, who is everything to us and who turns the very meagerness of our lives into enough and more. As the prayer chorus proclaims, "Christ is all, yes, all in all."

I like a story I heard about the great conductor of the NBC Symphony Orchestra, Arturo Toscanini. It happened one evening after he had exceeded even his own renowned brilliance in conducting Beethoven's great Ninth Symphony. The audience went wild; people stomped their feet, clapped and whistled. Toscanini bowed, again and again. He signaled to the orchestra and the chorus and the soloists, and they all stood to acknowledge the audience's exuberant gratitude. Eventually, the noise began to subside. With the quieting applause in the background, Toscanini turned and looked intently at the musicians and almost uncontrollably exclaimed, "Ladies and gentlemen!" The musicians leaned forward to listen. Why did the maestro seem so disturbed? Was he angry? Had someone missed a cue? Had the performance somehow been flawed?

No. Toscanini was not angry. Toscanini was stirred to the very depths of his being by the sheer magnificence of Beethoven's music. Scarcely able to talk, he whispered fiercely, "I am nothing." That was an extraordinary admission, since Toscanini was blessed with an enormous ego. Then he said to them, "You are nothing." That was hardly news. The musicians had often heard the same message in rehearsal. "But Beethoven," said Toscanini in a tone of high adoration, "Beethoven is everything, everything, everything!"

In a spirit of such adoring gratitude, we, like Simeon, lift up this Christ Child in our hearts and say, "Lord, my eyes have now seen Your salvation." Like those at the foot of the Cross, we gaze at a crucified Savior, high and lifted up, and we see our salvation in the wounded body of our Lord. The sacrifice fills our hearts with gratitude, and we pledge to live out our lives captive to it. So, we join George Herbert in his enduring prayer:

Thou hast given so much to me, Give me one thing more—
a grateful heart;
Not thankful when it pleaseth me as if Thy blessings had spare days;
But such a heart, whose pulse may be Thy praise! Amen.

May the vibrant pulse of your life and mine be the praising of our God, who never, ever fails us, even when we cannot see Him at work.

"May the God of hope fill you with all joy and peace in faith so that you overflow with hope by the power of the Holy Spirit" (Romans 15:13).

JANUARY 1 (NEW YEAR'S DAY)
Future Present: Living in the Hope

Scripture—Revelation 21:5

We usually begin the new year with good intentions. Whether or not we have a specific list of New Year's resolutions, we may hope to do better with our lives or perhaps our fortunes. We may be sufficiently satisfied if the new year proves not to be as bad as the one that just ended. We may hope to be better people in the new year. Many people do have a kind of clean-slate feeling, even a sense of a new start, as they begin a new year. At the least, most of us wonder what will be different in our world and in how we will live our lives in it.

In the December 16 meditation, we explored living life forward, letting the future spill over into the present, preparing ourselves now for the coming of the Kingdom of God in its fullness. In today's meditation, we will emphasize even more how each day has meaning for us if we allow God's Kingdom to affect how we live that day. This is living *in* the hope, not merely *with* the hope. Our hope is a point-blank confrontation carried out by Christians who refuse to compromise with the ways of hatred and unrighteousness, and who insist on living a holiness of radical compassion, righteousness and justice. Living in the hope is living the hope *now!*

For a follower of Jesus, hope is a strategy for today. You and I are the implementers of that strategy. Many Christians, however, have missed the point and settled into a comfortable complacency. They may wonder why God has waited so long to send Christ back for the Second Advent. They may have settled down and become willing waiters for Christ to come and clean up the world's mess, which they themselves have done little to clean up. Some have fallen prey to elaborate Last Times schemes, calming their uncertainty by embracing predictions based on questionable data, forced interpretations of Scripture, or some would-be modern prophet's claims. Predictably, the predictions never do pan out. It's worth our remembering that Jesus Himself claimed He didn't know the time of its coming either (Matthew 24:36).

I imagine God Himself is wondering why so many Christians are content to live in a cloud of despair and self-imposed powerlessness, while clinging to the prospect that someday, when God's Kingdom comes, their problems will be resolved, and life will be happy. Did they forget that Jesus announced the Kingdom *had* come and was already living among *them*, His disciples (Luke 17:21)? That the Kingdom was similar to living seeds someone else planted in the ground—seeds that His disciples were to nurture and harvest (Mark 4:26-29)? That they themselves were to be bearers of Gospel light—so convincing by their good works that others would see the glory of God in their midst (Matthew 5:16)? That in Revelation 21:5, John saw Jesus saying—in the *present tense*—"Look! I'm making all things new"? (The Second Advent/Coming is proclaimed in the *future tense* in the chapter that follows [22:7, 12].) Perhaps, the return of Christ has been delayed for so long, because we Christians have not taken the Kingdom of God seriously as a reality already implanted in the world by Jesus—a Kingdom in and by which He actually expects us to live our daily lives. We have copped out by postponing it and endlessly future-predicting it.

The good news is that the Kingdom is present today, and we have the privilege of living in it by following Jesus. He gives us the confidence to refuse to live by the loyalties and values of the present world order. He makes us equal to the soul-shaping challenge of choosing love over hate, humility over power addiction, reckless faith in Him over our timid plans, reconciliation over alienation. He shows us the way by gathering the poor and oppressed and inviting them to accept the privilege of living in a kingdom they never thought possible for the likes of them. He has the gall to love His enemies. He cowers before no earthly power. He loves those we wouldn't think deserve to be loved. He lives the Kingdom of God in a world order where it doesn't fit. And, He invites and trusts us to do the same, because, after all, He is our Rabbi, Teacher, Guide—after whom we as His disciples are called to model our lives.

Here are some prayer requests for the empowering and equipping we need to live in God's Kingdom today. Pray to receive courage—the kind behind Jeremiah's prophetic persistence in the face of endless rejection and persecution. Pray to receive a holy passion like that exuded by Martin Luther, John Calvin, and the Wesleys, who saw a corrupt and compromised Church and put their lives and reputations on the line to reform and renew it. Pray to receive a vision like that of William and Catherine Booth, who walked through the squalor of the East End of London, dared to see hope, and set out to bring some of God's Kingdom to such a seemingly unlikely place. Pray for compassion like that of Martin Luther King, Jr. and Mother Teresa, who risked their lives every day to advance the Beloved Community and to delegitimize every form of inhumanity. Live God's future *today!*

If you want this new year of your life to give God pleasure and make a significant contribution to the advancement of His

Kingdom, fully and prayerfully resolve to take the risk of actually living in His Kingdom. Don't make self-help resolutions—take revolutionary steps. Don't settle for a few little improvements here and there—take one or two steps that challenge the very order of the fallen world in which you live. Decide on one or two simple but radical changes you are going to make to confront the demons you are no longer willing to allow to hold sway in the world around you, or perhaps within you. If you and I do just one thing this year to challenge or upset the unrighteous order by which the world in which we live operates, we may well have given people a convincing glimpse of God's Kingdom. A "Happy New Year" for us disciples of Jesus is a year during which our unusual actions reveal to the world the power and beauty of the Kingdom of God—God's future in our present!

Prayer
Dear God, Lord of new beginnings, I enter this new year as a disciple of Your Jesus, wanting to bear a sufficient resemblance to Him to point others His way. I begin also as a builder of Your Kingdom, not to advance any cause or benefit of mine but to live courageously by Jesus' compassion for others, to walk in holiness of life, and to fight for the cause of righteousness. I ask You to arm me with courage, motivate me with Your love, and guide me with Your vision. May the life I live this year expose those whose lives I touch to the beauty and joy of Your Kingdom. I ask this in the name of Jesus, Your Son, Emmanuel, who brought us Your Kingdom and showed us how to live in it. Amen.

JANUARY 2

Uncommon Confidence: Living above Fear

Scripture—Judges 6:11-16a

Yesterday, we talked about bringing God's future into the present. We challenged ourselves to live our daily lives in ways that look like tomorrow's hope—in other words, to give a sufficiently convincing aroma and flavorful taste of God's coming Kingdom to stimulate others' appetites. This seems a tall order—and it is. Living by Kingdom values and ethics sometimes puts your life in stark contrast or even opposition to the present world order. We're being asked by Jesus to go against the grain for the sake of God's Kingdom. He warned us we'd face opposition. The odd reality of the beautiful Christlike life is that it is often seen as a threat by those who are living in self-centered complacency and exploitation.

We wouldn't be the first to be unsettled by the challenge. Time and again in Scripture, God called someone to a daunting task, and the person felt overwhelmed (Gideon), unqualified (Moses), or downright afraid (the disciples at Jesus' post-resurrection appearances). God did not, however, criticize the recipients of the challenge for feeling overwhelmed by what they were being called to do. Instead, He delivered what were the most important assuring words for the ones who are being tasked: *"I will be with you."* (You may remember that in an earlier meditation, we learned of some scholars who now believe that the very name for God revealed to Moses [*Yahweh*] means something along the lines of "I will be with you.") God is the One who is with those whom He calls and sends. He doesn't simply send us out cold; He sends us out with Him.

If you are a Christian, you are sent out by and with God, not alone. You are sent out by the One who goes with you. This has always been the case, beginning with the Old Testament. Low-feeling Gideon, for example, gained the courage and stamina to become Israel's leader, because, after clearly enumerating his disqualifications, he heard God dismiss them with a loud and clear "I will be with you." In the New Testament, the assurance doesn't change, but the nature of the accompaniment does. The assurance now comes in the form of Jesus. A new story began with the birth of Jesus. This Bethlehem-born, God-in-the-flesh-of-a-man is now the One who sends us out and goes with us. He models and teaches our mission for us—the details are in the Gospels. We have the helpful successes and instructive failures of the early Church mission in Acts and the Letters. And we have the insight into the future of the Church and the world in Revelation. This is the story we all fit into and the drama of which we are all called to be a part. We see in Scripture, and in particular the living and teaching of Jesus, the very life we are all sent out to live and the very mission on which we are sent. The question for us all is: How do I do it in my particular life situation? In the eyes of God, your particular calling is neither less nor more important than the calling of any other follower of Jesus. Where the Church has largely failed in its mission is where most Christians have left the challenge of Kingdom-of-God living to a few they consider the specially called, or the true saints, or those with spiritual depth. The New Testament makes it very clear that *all* followers of Jesus are called to be saints, holy ones, credible profiles of Jesus, and that they are called to accept that calling with confidence and to go about living it every day. God knows we won't do it perfectly every time. The important thing is to stay on a learning curve.

Every day, Jesus says to us, "I will be with you." It's not, however, a promise to name-only Christians—Christians who allow their fears to immobilize them into complacency. It's a promise for Christians who risk Kingdom-of-God living where they live. The true Church was built on such, and it will become a vital, transformative force for God's Kingdom today, when tribes of Christians will continue to live in this way with uncommon confidence in Christ's never-failing presence.

When we do live in this way, our Lord is with us in every possible situation in which we find ourselves. *He is there when things go wrong.* Job wondered about that when God allowed just about everything precious to be taken from him—not just his house and money, but his health and his family as well. Bad things happen to good people. In the depths of their suffering, sooner or later, they discover, like Job, truth beyond understanding. They see God clearer than ever. "*Now* my eyes have seen you," says Job to the Lord (Job 42:5b, italics added). His gracious presence is with us in the worst of circumstances.

He will also be there when we face tough decisions. The psalmist David was at a crossroads when he wrote to the Lord, "You are my hiding place; You will protect me from trouble and surround me with songs of deliverance." And then he heard God say to him, "I will instruct you and teach you in the way you should go; I will counsel you and watch over you" (Psalm 32:7-8). We must understand that this divine guidance isn't given in a spiritual vacuum. It becomes available when we spend time with our Lord. How can we expect clarity from Him if we only give Him quick visits? He is our divine Lover, and we are His beloveds. Lovers spend time together.

He will also be there when things go right. Success always has a downside. It tempts us to think we've arrived. It lures us toward complacency. "Isn't God blessing me/us in a wonderful way! I'm/we're in a really good place now. I've/we've arrived at my/our mountaintop and I'm/we're loving it!" Let us beware, lest our success lure us into a dangerous complacency, even a pious arrogance. Spiritual success is the gift of the Christ who accompanies and leads us, so it should humble us. Since it is always Christ's gift, we receive it well when we follow up by asking, "How can we boldly and compassionately advance the mission of Christ further with this gift?"

He will also be there tomorrow. We may be worried about our future, or what lies right around the corners of our lives. All of us face a tomorrow we cannot exactly predict. How do we live with the uncertainty and especially the fears we all have? We live courageously with the uncertainty and above the fears, because Jesus says, "I will be with you." We anticipate the future with uncommon confidence, because our trustworthy Jesus is there, calling us to Him.

Prayer

Dear God, I confess that sometimes my fears get the best of me. I'm too worried about what I don't know. I'm so tempted to expect the worst. I ask that You free me from the cowering that immobilizes my spirit and attacks my trust in You. Help me to see Your Christ more clearly, love Him more dearly, and follow Him more nearly. I ask this in His name—Christ, who sends me out as His disciple and goes with me all the way. Amen.

JANUARY 3

STRANGE CONFECTION: LIVING BLENDED LIVES

Scripture—Hebrews 12:1-17; James 1:9-12

For as long as I can remember, I've loved dark chocolate. This would explain what happened one day in my childhood. I happened into my mother's kitchen and saw a large bar of dark chocolate lying on the counter, waiting to be used, I assumed, in some recipe. Realizing I was alone, I broke off a large, bite-sized piece for myself. Having eagerly placed the piece in my mouth, anticipating a few moments of sheer delight, I was shocked by a bitterness greater than anything I had ever tasted. For a moment, I thought I'd been poisoned. I couldn't spit it out fast enough. Could such a bitter thing be an essential ingredient in a delicious cake icing? Keitha also makes a wonderful chocolate icing with semi-sweet chocolate (mmm…) and sour cream—but I would never think of consuming a bowl of nothing but sour cream! Ugh!

I've learned that a wonderful confection often contains at least one ingredient that is anything but tasty and can be downright awful. Scripture is like that. It's a confection of righteousness and love mixed with the bitter herbs of violence and sin, and still there emerges in its pages the undeserved texture and flavor of God's grace, confecting a wholeness, indeed a salvation. A person's life can be something beautiful, though it is a confection of very different experiences—some sweet and positive, others bitter and tragic.

The Christmas story itself is a confection. Consider the sweet ingredients:

- A glorious heavenly songster brigade filling the skies with their announcing praise
- A bright and beautiful star, showing the way to a Savior
- Men of wisdom from the East, not quite sure where their crazy faith is leading them, but trusting a sign
- A guy named Joseph, sorely tempted to back out of embarrassment, manning up and standing by his beloved Mary
- A teenager named Mary, saying "Yes" to improbability and allowing herself to be placed at the scary hub of salvation history

We must not, however, miss the bitter ingredients in the story:

- Temporarily homeless parents forced to have their unborn Child tough-journeyed to a place miles from home
- A crude and smelly stable
- Shepherds, the lowest of the low, in attendance
- A livestock's feeding trough for a cradle
- The evil plot of a power-seeking king to stop this birth from succeeding
- The parents and their newborn becoming refugees in Egypt
- A whole world shrouded in darkness and despair

It's a mixed bag, isn't it? There's some ugly stuff, along with the good stuff. And how do we usually handle the confection? Well, we tend to gravitate toward the good stuff. We celebrate the good news and pass over much of the unpleasantness, the ugliness, the violent politics, the stable-smelly side of Incarnation. No wonder Bing Crosby's Christmas song has endured as the most popular song of modern times. Yes, we long for that pristine, white Christmas when everything is just right, like a too-perfect December scene from Thomas Kinkade.

Truth be told, family arguments often happen during the Christmas season. Maybe there's an empty chair around the table for the first time. Perhaps, a job is lost or an illness changes just about everything, and Christmas isn't the same. It's as if the more special the season, the more things can go wrong, including Christmas dinner.

So, what shall we make of this mixed bag of a season—and of our lives, for that matter? I think the Christmas story is inviting us to take everything, the good and the bad experiences, the mountaintop highs and the deep-valley lows, the triumphs and the tragedies, the successes and the failures, the affirmations and the hurts—all of it—and let God confect it into something beautiful, like delicious chocolate cake made with the sweet, along with the bitter.

Is there a basic recipe our Lord follows in His confections? Yes, and no. Yes, He has a *standard* recipe for all of us. The ingredients are love, grace, mercy, forgiveness, power to do the right, hope, comfort and joy. But each of us is so different from everyone else. And each of us has experienced some things in a unique way. And so, for each of us, He also has a *secret* recipe. Most cooks and chefs have their own secret recipes for particular dishes. My mother made the most perfect pecan pie: deeply delicious and rich, and yet seemingly so light. Before she passed away, she was nice enough to leave her secret, hand-written recipe for Keitha and my sister Miriam, who followed it diligently. Their efforts, however, did not have quite the same results. It took time for them to figure out what the written recipe had omitted, and now they both make superb pecan pie. That unique pecan pie of Florence, my mother, now lives on in my mind and taste buds as the best ever.

Each one of us is in a class by him- or herself. Each of our lives is a unique confection of sweets and bitters, goods and bads. The question is: Who is the confectioner we can trust? Who can hold it all in big enough hands? Who is the Divine Confectioner who can work by grace the confection that is *your* life, mix it gently, sometimes painfully, apply the right heat, follow the right timing—*on the way to the uniquely beautiful thing your life can become?*

The Christmas season is not about pretty things, expensive gifts, everything coming-up-roses—"the most wonderful time of the year" in every way. It's far better than that. It's about the beginning of a beautiful *life*, a life birthed in a world of good and bad, holiness and horror, hope and despair. A life unlike any other, taking in the good given to it and also the bad inflicted upon it, and confecting the beautiful, beloved Jesus. A life of holiness, love and the Kingdom of God. You and I are the beneficiaries of this Divine Confection we call Gospel.

The thing is this—the Christmas thing, that is. If we let ourselves brave the dark night of our winter, as well as receive the undeserved graces and gifts God sends our way, He will invite us to walk alongside Jesus, from cradle to grave, in and into eternity. And whoever you are, yours will be a beautiful life—or we could say, an irresistible confection of amazing grace.

Prayer

Thank you, Lord, for the wonderful blessings and gifts You give me daily. Thank You also for not coddling me with endless positive experiences and weakening me with anxious protectiveness. Thank You, as well, for giving me the grace and strength to cope with the threats, losses and attacks that come my way. I now ask that You take it all and confect of my life something that gives witness to Your power to make beauty out of the mixed bag of a life, through Jesus Christ my Lord. Amen.

JANUARY 4

Christlike Humility: Living without Illusion

Scripture—John 13:12-15; Philippians 2:1-8; Romans 12:3

In a world captivated by materialism and self-advancement, the real Christmas story is a shocker. It says that God, who is "high and lifted up," did something that turns our view of Him on its head. It says He came to Earth in human flesh. He became a human (John 1:14). He radically downsized. Somehow, "high and lifted up" had to make room for "humble and lowered down" (Philippians 2:7).

In the Christian Church—and in many other religious communities as well—people speak, sing, teach and preach God's greatness. They are right to do so. They are probably thinking in terms of the mind-boggling complexity and breathtaking beauty of the endless universe God has created and still is creating. They may also be thinking of the greatness of His grace—a grace that looks down upon us with such undeserved favor. Or they may have in mind His love, which is broad enough to reach us all. The Christmas story, however, gives witness to what I believe is the crowning miracle of God's greatness: *He became small.*

God's condescension is probably the most forgotten or ignored miracle in the Gospel. That is quite understandable in a world that doesn't like to think small. Where does this self-lowering God fit into this self-enhancing culture of ours? What can this God offer a world caught up in its obsessive fascination with bigger and better? And perhaps more importantly, what does He offer the left-behinds in such a world?

He offers a very different way of life called *humility*, a holy humanness that rejects both the desperate striving of those who always want more and the self-demeaning of those who see themselves as the losers. Both are living a tragic illusion.

What exactly was God doing when He became a human? To put it simply, He was freeing us to become humans. A human being is who God created you and me to be! Those who think our problem or our sin is that "we're only human" are sadly mistaken. The glory God has given us is *the glory of being fully human*. Our sin is our presuming to be something else, something greater, or lesser. Our sin is to live such a lie.

God became a small infant named Jesus to invite us to discover the beauty and the holiness of our true humanity. He was born poor and stayed poor to expose the dehumanizing seduction of wealth. He avoided making Himself famous, built no political power base, and became a failure by contemporary standards in order to delegitimize the lust for power. He stayed within a relatively obscure and insignificant part of the great Roman Empire and spent most of His time with the marginalized, so that He could affirm their full worth. He allowed the power of a crowd, an empire and a religious establishment to deliver Him to a criminal's crucifixion. He put Himself alongside the worst of us, just in case there was anyone who thought God was too much above them. He became small to show us who we are. We are neither greater nor lesser than human. We are human, created in His image. Those who think they are greater have exaggerated themselves; those who think they are lesser have demeaned themselves. Neither is true humility.

I am convinced there is only one way some can be saved from the empty, self-centered greatness they are pursuing. There is only one way they can be freed from the captive hold it has on them. It is to find a different greatness—the different greatness of God, who becomes small Himself and offers all of us the same greatness—the greatness of His humility. The path of God downward is the path to which He calls the proud.

I'm also convinced there is only one way others can be saved from the insidious grip of their self-demeaning outlooks and attitudes. And that is to see that Jesus considers no one as beneath Himself, no one as a lesser, no one as incapable of being one of His adopted. Low self-esteem is as sinful as excessive self-esteem. To demean what God has created in His own image is to demean God.

Jesus gives you and me the gift of humility. We may not have discovered it. This gift is an open door to who we really are. If we choose to live in a grasping presumption, we will be perpetually dissatisfied. On the other hand, if we demean ourselves and expect that nothing we do will have real value, we will diminish our true humanity. Humility is a way of life that avoids both terrible mistakes. The humble, like Christ, know who they are. They neither inflate nor deflate themselves. They live in the joy of their humanity. They do not think more highly of themselves than they ought to think, nor more lowly of themselves than they ought. If you strive for greatness in the eyes of others, you need to find your true greatness in the eyes of the God who redeemed you to be the unique human being He created you to be. If you have given yourself over to self-belittlement, you need to claim your true identity and importance as a son or daughter of the God who created and redeemed you in His image. The truly humble have said goodbye to both self-promotion and self-demotion. They are truly Christlike.

Christ frees us to live in the joy of who we really are. What the birth of Jesus inaugurated, what His ministry taught us, and what His life, death and resurrection unleashed, is the possibility of being the humans God created us to be. We discover who we really are when we come to God in humility, surrendering our pretensions or our too low self-esteem, whichever the case may be, and divesting ourselves of such illusions about ourselves. Then, for the first time perhaps, we find our true souls, the very center of who we really are, the image of Himself that God has implanted in us.

For this, God humbled Himself, so *we* could become human again.

Prayer

Thank You, Lord, for meeting us at our level and showing us the way of humility. I want so much to be like You. I want to see and be who I really am as Your follower and student. If I have bought into any illusions about my self-importance or sought my self-worth in my accomplishments, please bring me down to the earth from which You fashioned me. Or if I have concocted any falsehood about my inferiority compared to others or believed that I have been cursed with worthlessness, please bring me up from this pit of pity to live with You on the level playing field of Your accepting and empowering love. I ask this in the name of Jesus, who became one of us to help us become our true selves. Amen.

JANUARY 5

Deep Joy: Living in the Surprises of God

Scripture—Luke 2:10, 20; John 15:9-11

For many, the Christmas season has been spent running after imagined promises of joy, and now the joy has gone, or it never came to pass. The real message of Christmas joy was probably not heard or received in the first place. It was confiscated and corrupted by shallow fixes. Christmas has been spent chasing after something called "the holiday spirit"—the joy and the merriment that is supposed to come with the season. When it's all over, however, these chasers after happiness now wonder what there really was to be happy about. They've spent the season and their fair share of money trying to manufacture joy, only to find the sadness hasn't left them.

The joy which the Christmas story embodies is not a joy that needs pursuing. It is deep joy, and it is a gift. It cannot be manufactured by our calculations and planning. A well planned party doesn't guarantee it, nor does a delightful Christmas play or concert. Deep joy is a gift given by God, beginning with the Babe in a Bethlehem manger that sent awkward shepherds singing and dancing on the way home, and sophisticated Magi uncharacteristically rejoicing and going on their knees with hearts full and overflowing.

Such joy cannot be taken; it can only be received. As Ecclesiastes reminds us again and again, the search for a personal happiness ends in failure. Joy is a gift to be received with empty hands and a willing heart.

Neither can this joy be kept privately; it can only be multiplied publicly. It must be shared with others. God doesn't give us possessions to keep to ourselves; He gives us gifts to give away. We are called to go viral with the joy. The early Salvationists, who had meager worldly goods, were notorious for their extreme expressions of overflowing joy. Many years later, at a centennial celebration in London, the Archbishop of Canterbury could still say publicly to Queen Elizabeth II, "Your Majesty, I have never met a glum Salvationist!" Evidently, the joy was still overflowing. Is it still?

Deep joy only comes one way: God delivers it, and He defines it. We cannot figure out what we think makes us happy, and then expect that God will do precisely that favor for us. We aren't that smart about what exactly will bring us deep joy. Furthermore, we would probably tend to ask for joys that demand little of us. The joy God gives, however, isn't a warm, cozy feeling. It will, more often than not, make us shake in our boots. If that sounds strange, remember that when the angel told Mary the good news that she would bear the Messiah, and later appeared to the shepherds inviting them to see this newborn Messiah, he also told them not to be afraid. Why should they be afraid of this good news? Answer: because it would affect their lives in ways they had never imagined. They would have to change.

We need not be afraid of this new, deeper joy. The joy God brings to us, however, also awakens the coward in us. Our internal coward suddenly realizes that if we receive this joy that God gives us in Jesus, we can no longer be the same. Mary had to face the awesome task of bearing and nurturing the Messiah, and later the perplexity His mission would cause her and the pain His early, torturous death would inflict on her. The shepherds had to turn the carnality of their shepherdly existence into a divine vocation of radiant dignity. Magi would have to throw away their philosophical systems and reconstruct their whole way of thinking about life, based on the incredible place and Person to which their star journey had led them. For you and me today, the deep joy of Christ propels us out of the old molds of our safe, boring existence and takes us on a joy ride of Christ-led adventure. And either the coward in us wins out, throwing us back to safety, or we say to our Lord, "Let's go," and He says to us, "Hang on!"

The follower of Jesus is not called to live a dull, predictable life. Jesus makes no allowance for it. Excitement and joy prance through the pages of the New Testament like Christmas reindeer. Jesus says nothing about the Kingdom of God that gives license to boredom and misery. Rather, the intention of His teaching is to instill His joy in us, so that our joy will be complete (John 15:11), and so that we can share completely in His joy (17:13b).

Don't get me wrong. It's not all a joy ride. Deep sorrows come. What happens to the joy then? Well, it doesn't disappear. It goes deeper, and when the time comes, it emerges with new strength as God surprises us again. The Resurrection was God's surprise hidden in the Crucifixion. The persecution of Christians, says James, will mold a steadfast character and make us more complete (James 1:3-4). The loss of a loved one will give us a new depth and encourage us to move on to a new level and find new strength. Sorrows have hidden gifts which God wants to give when we're ready. Preparing His disciples for His death, Jesus said, "Your will be sorrowful, but your sorrow will turn into joy" (John 16:20b). The reality, said the apostle Paul, is that nothing in all creation will be able to separate us from God's love in Christ Jesus our Lord (Romans 8:38-39)—our ultimate joy.

There is an important secret to living our lives in this deep joy: *Trust God to surprise you.* God is not predictable; otherwise He would not be God—He would be a reliable formula, or a preprogrammed heavenly robot, or an easily manipulated divine parent. God doesn't play tricks on us, but He does love to give us gifts (blessings) beyond anything we could ever predict or force from Him. Nevertheless, He does allow the rain to fall on both those who love Him and those who don't. He allows bad stuff to happen to all of us. But somewhere along the way, He pulls a surprise on us. He delivers joy, a deeper joy, a joy no circumstance or person can take from us. And we learn that our God means us no ill. On the contrary, He means us the joy that lasts. Through His Spirit, He draws closer, and we feel His embrace. He surprises us with His extraordinary love and touches us with His undeserved grace. And in the deeper joy this brings, we discover the sheer delight of living in the surprises of our God.

Prayer
Dear Lord, help me to realize that what I call surprising blessings from You are, for You, the normal expressions of Your love for us. I confess that I have sometimes doubted You, because something did not work out in the way I thought You should have made it work out. Please forgive me for presuming to know what You should do or how You should express Your love. Please help me to release my tight grip on life, so that You can teach me how deep joy comes with surrendering to You, trusting You, and looking for the surprises from You that make life so incredibly delightful and rewarding. I ask this in the name of Jesus, Your greatest and most rewarding surprise for the world. Amen.

"You are the light of the world ... Let your light shine before people, so they can see the good things you do and praise your Father who is in Heaven" (Matthew 5:14a, 16).

JANUARY 6 (EPIPHANY)
Star Journey: Living Brightly in the Darkness

Scripture—Matthew 2:1-12; II Corinthians 4:5-6; Philippians 2:14-15

The day the Christian Church calls Epiphany (always January 6th) was named after the Greek word that meant "appearance" or "manifestation." Today, we sometimes use the word to express some new insight or idea that suddenly dawns upon us—like a scientist stumbling upon a new theory, or any of us suddenly becoming aware of a new reality or dimension in our lives. "Today, I had an epiphany!" we may exclaim in light of a revelation. The word carries the sense of something we didn't know before that has been unexpectedly revealed.

The Bible is full of epiphanies, such as Old Testament prophets receiving startling new messages from the Lord, disciples hearing radically new teachings from their Rabbi Jesus, or the spiritual explosion of insight and empowerment at Pentecost. The epiphany we look to today is the epiphany that claims our vision. It invites us to come see Jesus. It asks us to follow Him for the rest of our lives. For those of us who are already His followers, epiphany invites us to reclarify the direction of our lives or even set out in a new direction.

Epiphany begins as *mystery*. The Magi of Matthew 2 weren't following their calculations based on astrological science. They were following what they didn't understand, what their science couldn't explain. They were following a mystery. Epiphany is something we can't fully get our minds around. It is something that gets around us, envelops us, holds us if we let it, changes us, beginning with our hearts. Epiphany is God beckoning us to the mystery, the unknown place, the calling which we don't yet fully grasp. It asks of us a new beginning, or perhaps yet another new beginning. Beyond logic, it is truth that captures our hearts.

One lone night almost two thousand years ago, an unusual star appeared. Thousands must have seen the same star, maybe even wondered about a particularly direct beam it seemed to throw to Earth. But only a few Magi thought it could point to something profoundly significant, something they could not explain by their science. Could it be to a place where something might happen to change their lives—and even the world? An epiphany that came from a different source outside the careful calculations they had achieved and for which they had been recognized in the scientific and religious communities? Can you imagine the professional risk they were taking when they cast their lot with this strange star?

The scenes in their homes must have been interesting. Imagine them packing for the trip and their wives trying to get a little more information. "Tell me again, dear, where you're going, and why? . . . . Oh! . . . . I see." Then to the children: "Don't bother your father. He's been under a lot of stress this year. He . . . . he needs to get away for a few days . . . . or weeks."

Their neighbors probably weren't as kind: "What kind of wild goose chase are these guys on? Imagine them leaving their families and responsibilities to follow some stray star! I've heard a lot of crackpot stories to excuse deserting your family, but this one takes the cake!"

And so, the Magi set out, with a guiding star before them and gawking stares behind them, to follow the epiphany, wherever it led them.

Have you ever found yourself in a somewhat similar situation where you may have been handed some God-given clue to a direction of your life, and you failed to see it at the time? Has Christ ever come near and you did not allow yourself to hear what He had say, or you failed to heed where He wanted to lead you? Were you just not looking or listening? Or am I the only one?

This *Advent* season, we prepared ourselves to receive the Christ. This *Christmas* season, we began to explore some of the ways we now live our lives in the world which God entered in Jesus of Nazareth, and where He is still present and active through His Holy Spirit. Now, on this day of *Epiphany*, we become Magi. We ask God for a promising star, a beam of revelation, a hint of the future into which He wants to lead us.

As the Magi followed the star westward, it seemed to be leading to Jerusalem. They knew enough about the Jews to know the importance of this city to the Jewish faith. Herod the Great had, in fact, started the construction of a new Jewish temple in this capital city, and Jews thought it was all in preparation for a new Messianic Age. Yes, this made absolute sense: The King of the Jews would *have* to be born in the capitol of the Jewish faith.

"Wrong," said the chief priests and teachers of the law. "The prophet Micah said, 'in Bethlehem Ephrathah . . . the least significant of Judah's forces' (Micah 5:2)." "Where's that?" "Oh, just down the road to the south. Small town. Not much there. But if you do find something, let us know." "Bethlehem? We've come all this way to go to some little cow town?"

Well, they arrived in Bethlehem and started looking around. The radiance seemed to be taking them to the outskirts. "What's that? A cow stall?" Well, yes, cow towns would have a few cow stalls. "And we're supposed to find what we're looking for there? *This* is the conclusion of our journey?"

Actually, it was the beginning. They found the cow stall that seemed to be drawing the beam of star light. They entered. "It's a cow stall alright—even smells like one. Glad we brought the incense...." They come closer, stare in wonder. "No, no.... Glad we brought *ourselves*.... Let's worship."

Do you want to follow God's Epiphany star? Are you ready to embrace the Child and follow where He leads? Be aware: it may not take you to where you want to go. In fact, it probably won't, because it will take you *through* the Jerusalems, on down the road to the little Bethlehems, to where the *real* miracles are—all the places human pride causes us to look down on.

If you settle in Jerusalem, you follow your own star. You're looking for your own big chance to "make it"—because, as they say, if you can make it in Jerusalem, you can make it anywhere! And you may even find a little happiness for the time being, but your star will sooner or later burn and fall.

Epiphany invites us to follow another star, the one that leads us to Bethlehem. Follow the one that shines on humble people, the one that illumines the unlikely places where Jesus is most at home. We can't miss the irony of the Magi, foreigners of privilege and wealth (How else could they afford the luxury of full-time star gazing and universe speculation?) falling on their knees on dirty straw and worshiping a baby born into poverty. Their science didn't bring them there. A mysterious epiphany begging for exploration did. A hope and a trust that the light might bring them to divinity, to the end of their life's search for faith, meaning and purpose.

We hear no more about those Magi in Scripture, although legends abound. One legend gave each one a name and a description. Another legend had it that after many years, they were visited by the apostle Thomas, who gave them specific instructions and mentoring, and eventually made them bishops in the Eastern Church. What we can say is that Matthew would only have included the story of their star journey if he knew that their lives were deeply changed and that they became ardent followers of Jesus, the very first disciples from a foreign land. They are the ones who began scattering the light beyond the narrow borders of Palestine.

The challenge of the Magi is twofold: worship only the One to whom the Light brings us, and then live brightly in the darkness. This is exactly where Christmas brings us. Keep in mind that during the day, stars are mostly invisible. They can only shine in all their brilliance in the night. Yes, we followers of Jesus are called to enjoy and strengthen the benefits of our Jesus faith in the company of one another; this is an important part of being the Church. The *most* important part of being the Church, however, is living the life and spreading the light of Jesus in the world—the place where we are the Church in radiant contrast to the darkness. This is the only way the world will come to faith. Are you on board?

Prayer
Dear God of Light, in whom is no darkness, help me to shine in this dark world with the glow of Your glory and the reflection of Your likeness. Give me the star-studded courage of those Magi. Help me to live a life that marries worship and witness. Help me to believe and prove Your truth, even though I can't always get my mind around it.

I now embark again on a journey with You to discover new places that need Your light, or perhaps to reenter the place where I already live, only now to light it up with the life of Jesus. I ask this in the name of Jesus, the Lord of my journey and the Star I follow. Amen.

WORKS CITED

Carroll, James. *Christ Actually: The Son of God for the Secular Age*. New York: Viking Penguin, 2014.

Dionne, E.J., Jr. "God, as We Hadn't Seen Him." *Atlanta Journal-Constitution* (Dec. 25, 2003).

Frost, Robert. "The Wind and the Rain," *The Poetry of Robert Frost*. New York: Henry Holt and Company, 1969.

Johnson, Josephine W. *Now in November*. New York: Simon and Schuster, 1970.

Plantinga, Cornelius, Jr. "Between Two Advents: In the Interim." *Christian Century* (Dec. 6, 2000).

Salinger, J.D. *Catcher in the Rye*. Boston: Little, Brown and Company, 1951.

The Salvation Army Song Book (SASB). Alexandria, VA: The Salvation Army, National Headquarters, 2015.

Willimon, William H. *Christian Century* (Nov. 23, 1988).

A BRIEF GLOSSARY

(For the benefit of readers not familiar with certain Salvation Army terms that appear in this book)

Adult Rehabilitation Center—a Salvation Army residential ministry for people addicted to drugs and/or alcohol. The rehab program combines spiritual development, group meetings, and work therapy.

Camp Grandview—one of many summer camps and year-round conference centers operated by TSA.

Corps—a local Salvation Army missional church.

The mercy seat—the kneeling rail to which worshipers are invited to come forward to pray, usually following the sermon.

Salvation Army officers—men and women ordained and commissioned to serve and lead the Salvation Army's mission.

Salvationism—expressing one's Christian faith as part of TSA and its mission.

Salvationist—a person who serves the mission of Christ as a participant in TSA in the world.

Salvationist Doctrines—the eleven articles of faith that articulate key doctrines of TSA.

Training College—a two-year residential preparatory course of study and practice for Salvation Army officers.